The
Colonial Cavalier
or
Southern Life
Before the Revolution

Maud Wilder Goodwin

Illustrated by *Harry Edwards*

HERITAGE BOOKS
2010

HERITAGE BOOKS
AN IMPRINT OF HERITAGE BOOKS, INC.

Books, CDs, and more—Worldwide

For our listing of thousands of titles see our website
at
www.HeritageBooks.com

A Facsimile Reprint
Published 2010 by
HERITAGE BOOKS, INC.
Publishing Division
100 Railroad Ave. #104
Westminster, Maryland 21157

Copyright © 1894 United States Book Company

Index Copyright © 2010 Heritage Books, Inc.

— Publisher's Notice —
In reprints such as this, it is often not possible to remove blemishes from the original. We feel the contents of this book warrant its reissue despite these blemishes and hope you will agree and read it with pleasure.

International Standard Book Numbers
Paperbound: 978-0-7884-5229-1
Clothbound: 978-0-7884-8506-0

Contents

	PAGE
Preface,	7
His Home,	13
Sweethearts and Wives,	43
His Dress,	73
News, Trade and Travel,	97
His Friends and Foes,	125
His Amusements,	141
His Man-Servants and His Maid-Servants,	165
His Church,	189
His Education,	221
Laws, Punishments and Politics,	243
Sickness and Death,	273

Preface

TWO great forces have contributed to the making of the Anglo-American character. The types, broadly classed in England as Puritan and Cavalier, repeated themselves in the New World. On the bleak Massachusetts coast, the Puritan emigrants founded a race as rugged as their environment. Driven by the force of compelling conscience from their homes, they came to the new land, at once pilgrims and pioneers, to rear altars and found homes in the primeval forest. It was not freedom of worship alone they sought, but their own way. They found it and kept it. Such a race produced a strong and hardy type of manhood, admirable if not always lovable.

But there was another force at work, moulding the national character, a force as persistent, a type as intense as the Puritan's own, and its exact opposite. The men who settled the Southern Colonies, Virginia, Maryland, and the Carolinas, were Cavaliers; not necessarily in blood, or even in loyalty to the Stuart cause, but Cavalier in sympathies, in the general view of life, in virtues and vices. So

PREFACE.

far as the provinces could represent the mother country, Virginia and Maryland reflected the Cavaliers, as Massachusetts and Connecticut reflected the Puritans.

Their settlers came, impelled by no religious motives, and driven by no persecution. They lacked, therefore, the bond of a common enthusiasm and the still stronger tie of a common antipathy. Above all, they lacked the town-meeting. Separated by the necessities of plantation life, they formed a series of tiny kingdoms rather than a democratic community. To the Puritan, the village life of Scrooby and its like was familiar and therefore dear; but to the Southern settlers, the ideal was the great estate of the English gentry whose descendants many of them were.

The term, "Cavalier," came into vogue in the struggle between Charles the First and his Parliament, but the type itself was already well-developed in the reign of James, and under the fostering influence of Buckingham. A great deal of energy has been wasted in the discussion as to how much of this Cavalier blood was found among the early settlers. It is enough that we know that, between the coming of the first adventurers and the Restoration, the number of " gentlemen" was sufficient to direct the policy of the State, and color the life of its society.

PREFACE.

When the earliest colonists left England, the Cavalier was at the height of his glory. Now he represents a lost cause, "and none so poor to do him reverence." The sceptre of royal authority is shattered; society has grown dull and decorous. Even in dress, the Puritan has prevailed. The people who speak of Cromwell's followers as "Roundheads" and "Cropped Ears," go closer cropped than they, and the costume of a gentleman of to-day is uglier and gloomier than any the Puritan ever dreamed of introducing.

These concessions of the modern world make the Puritan a familiar figure, as he stands out in the page of Hawthorne, or on the canvas of Boughton. But the Cavalier fades into the dim and shadowy background of the past. We cannot afford to have him slip away from us so, if we wish really to understand the history of our country; we must know both sides of its development.

Hitherto, the real comprehension of the Colonial Cavalier has been hindered by the florid enthusiasm of the South, and the critical coldness of the North. His admirers have painted him as a theatrical personage, always powdered and beruffled, fighting duels as frequently as he changed his dress, living in lordly state in a baronial mansion, or dancing in the brilliant halls of fashion in the season at the capital. All this is, of course,

PREFACE.

seen to be absurd, as one comes to study the conditions under which he lived. We find the "capital" a straggling village, the "estate" a half-cultivated farm, and the "host of retainers" often but a mob of black slaves, clad in motley, or lying half-naked in the sun. Does it follow, then, that the lives of these men are not worth serious study? Surely not. It is in the very primitiveness of environment that the chief interest of the study of that early life lies. Here were men who brought to the New World a keen appreciation of the luxuries and refined pleasures of life, who had not eschewed them for conscience's sake like the Puritan, yet who relinquished them all bravely and cheerfully, to face the hardships and dangers of a pioneer life; and when their descendants, growing rich with the increasing prosperity of the country, had once more surrounded themselves with beautiful homes and wide acres, they too stood ready to sacrifice them all at the call of Liberty. If we would understand Washington, and Jefferson, and the Lees, George Mason, and John Randolph, we must study them as the "Autocrat" tells us we should all be studied, for at least a century before birth.

The Colonial Cavalier must be painted, like a Rembrandt, with high lights and deep shadows. It is idle to ignore his weaknesses or his vices.

PREFACE.

They are of the kind that insist on notice. Yet, with all his faults, he will surely prove well worth our serious consideration, and however wide we open our eyes to his defects, however we seek to brush away the illusions with which tinsel hero-worship has surrounded him, we shall still find him, judged as he has a right to be, at his best, closely approaching Lowell's definition of a gentleman: "A man of culture, a man of intellectual resources, a man of public spirit, a man of refinement, with that good taste which is the conscience of the mind, and that conscience which is the good taste of the soul."

This little volume makes no pretensions to the dignity of a history. It aims only, through local gossip and homely details of life and customs, to open a side-door, through which we may, perchance, gain a sense of fireside intimacy with *The Colonial Cavalier*.

His Home

The Colonial Cavalier

His Home

I STOOD in the wide hall of the old brick mansion built, a century and a half ago, by "King Carter," on the shore of the James River.

It was Autumn. The doors at either end of the saloon were open, and their casements framed the landscape like a picture. From the foot of the moss-grown steps at the rear, the drive stretched its length, under several closed gates, for half a mile, till it joined the little travelled high-road. From the porch in front, the ground fell away, in what had once been a series of terraces, to the brink of the river, across whose western hills the November sun was setting red. Not a ripple stirred the surface of the water—the dead leaves on the ground never rustled. All was still; solitary, yet not melancholy. The place seemed apart from the present—a part of the past.

Within doors, everything was mellowed by the

softening touch of twilight and age. The hospitable fire which blazed in the great throat of the library chimney, cast odd shadows on the high wainscot, and the delicately wrought mouldings over the chimney-breast, and its reflections danced in the small panes of the heavily framed windows as though the witches were making tea outside.

The dark staircase wound upward in the centre of the hallway, its handrail hacked by the swords of soldiers in the Revolution. As I glanced at it, and then out along the long avenue, I seemed to see Tarleton's scarlet-clad dragoons dashing up to surround the house. Then, as I turned westward, imagination travelled still further into the past, and pictured the slow approach of a British packet, gliding peacefully up to the little wharf down yonder, to discharge its household freight of tea and spices, of India muslins and "callamancoes" before it proceeded on its way to the town of Williamsburg, a few miles farther up the river.

At the period of which I was dreaming, Williamsburg was the capital of the province, with a wide street named in honor of the Duke of Gloucester, and a college named after their late majesties, William and Mary, with a jolly Raleigh tavern and a stately Governor's Palace; but all this had come about some fifty years before the building of *Carter's Grove*.

Hall in
Carter's Grove
James River, Va.

THE COLONIAL CAVALIER.

In the middle of the seventeenth century it was far more primitive,—indeed, it was not Williamsburg at all, but only "The Middle Plantation," with a few pioneer houses surrounded by primeval forests, from which savage red faces now and then peered out, to the terror of the settlers; while at nightfall the heavy wooden shutters had been closed, lest the firelight should prove a shining mark for the Indian's arrow. If the traveller found Williamsburg in the eighteenth century "a straggling village," and its mansions "houses of very moderate pretensions," what would he have thought of those first modest homes, where the horse-trough was the family wash-basin; where stools and benches, hung against the wall, constituted the furniture; where the kitchen-table served for dining-table as well, and was handsomely set out with bowls, trenchers, and noggins of wood, with gourds and squashes daintily cut, to add color to the meal; while the family was counted well off that could muster a few spoons, and a plate or two of shining pewter! But those pioneers and their wives felt pride in their little homes, for they realized how favorably they contrasted with the cabins built at "James Cittie" by Wingfield and Smith and their fellow-adventurers. They had indeed more cause for honest pride than the stay-at-homes in England could ever realize, for such knew nothing of the infinite toil and the difficulty of founding a settlement in a new country, thousands of miles from civilization, with forests to be cleared and savages to be fought, turbulent followers to be ruled, and food, shelter, and clothing to be provided.

No sooner were the "Ancient Planters," as the chronicles call the first settlers, fairly ashore on their island, than the Company at home opened its battery of advice upon them: "Seeing order is at the same price with confusion," the secretary wrote, setting down a very dubious proposition as an aphorism, "it shall be advisably done to set your houses even and by a line, that your streets may have a good breadth, and be carried square about your market-place, and every street's end opening into it, that from thence, with a few field-pieces, you may command every street throughout; which market-place you may also fortify, *if you think it needful.*" It must have seemed grimly humorous to those pioneers, huddling their cabins together within the shelter of the wooden fence, dignified by the name of a palisade, and mounted with all the guns they could muster, to be thus advised from a distance of three thousand miles to construct at once a model English village, and fortify the market-place, *if they thought best.* An Italian proverb has it that "it is easy to threaten a bull from a window," and so the Virginia Company found no difficulty in regulating the affairs of the colonists and the Indians, from their window in London. The settlers paid as little heed as possible to their interference, and struggled on through the sickness and the starving-time, as best they could, clearing away the brush, and felling trees, and putting up houses. But building went on so slowly that in 1619, "In James Cittie were only those houses that Sir Thomas Gates built in the tyme of his government (1610), with one wherein the governor allwayes dwelt, and a church built wholly at the charge of the inhabitants of the citye, of timber, being fifty foote in length and twenty in breadth." The report from the town of Henrico was still less encouraging, for there were found only "three old houses, a poor ruinated church, with some few poore buildings on the islande."

Yet, in spite of hindrances and drawbacks, the colony prospered. Lord De la Warre reported that all the enterprise needed was "a few honest laborers burdened with children"; and such alluring inducements were held out to immigrants, that I cannot understand how the London poor, swarming in their black alleys, could resist the invitation to come over to a land where pure air and plenty were to be had for nothing. Ralph Hamor wrote home: "The affairs of the colony being so well ordered and the hardest tasks already overpast, that whosoever, now or hereafter, shall happily arrive there, shall finde a handsome house of some four roomes or more, if he have a family, to repose himselfe in, rent-free, and twelve English acres of ground adjoining thereunto, very strongly impailed; which ground is only allotted unto him for roots, gardaine-herbs and corne; neither shall he need to provide himselfe victuals. He shall have for himselfe and family a competent twelve-months' provision delivered unto him." In addition to all this, the colonist was to be furnished with tools of all sorts, and "for his better subsistence, he shall have poultry and swine, and if he prefer, a goate or two, and perhaps a cowe given him." I am at a loss to understand why all England did not emigrate at once to the land where such a gift-enterprise was on foot. Perhaps the readers distrusted Hamor's authority; perhaps they thought some extraordinary risks or dangers must lurk behind such fair promises, and when the Indian massacre came, they possibly nodded their wise heads and said, "I told you so."

The agent of the Maryland Company worked on a very different system from this gilded Virginia offer. He published a pamphlet giving detailed directions to "intending settlers." They were not

to depend on the resources of the colony, even for the first year, but to bring with them laborers and watch-dogs, grains and seeds of all kinds, and meal enough to last while their houses were a-building.

I find that I gain the best idea of what these first houses in America were like, by asking myself how I should have built, in the conditions under which the settlers worked, dropped down in a little forest-clearing, the ocean before and the Indians behind, with few and imperfect tools, and with a pressure all the while of securing food for to-day, and sowing grain for to-morrow. I am sure I should have put up a shelter of the rudest kind that could be trusted to withstand the winds of Autumn, and the storms of Winter. I should not have planed my beams, nor matched my floor-boards. Only my doors and shutters I should have made both strong and stout, to meet the gales from the sea, or a sudden dash from lurking savages in the bush. This I find, therefore, without surprise, was just what the settlers did. They divided the house into a kitchen and a bedroom, with a shed joined on for the goats and pigs, or, if the owner were so lucky, a cow. Their chimneys were chiefly constructed out of twigs plastered on both sides with clay, which dried in the sun, and served for some time, before it crumbled again to dust. As there were no mills, the corn-grinding had to be done at home; so the settlers, learning the trick from the Indians, improvised a mortar, by burning out the stump of a tree into a hollow, and hanging over it a log, suspended from the limb of a tree close at hand, for a pestle. This was hard work, and the grinding in the little hand-mills brought from England was scarcely easier. A dying man, leaving his children to their uncle's care, expressly stipulated that they should not be put to the drudgery of pounding corn.

Within the house, stood the great and small wheels for wool and flax, the carding-comb and

the moulds for making those candles, of green myrtleberry wax which, as Beverly writes, "are never greasie to the touch, nor melt with lying in the hottest weather. Neither does the snuff of these ever offend the smell, like that of a tallow-candle; but instead of being disagreeable, if an accident puts a candle out, it yields a pleasant fragrancy to all that are in the room, insomuch that nice people often put them out on purpose to have the incense of the expiring snuff."

It was no pitiable life that those pioneers lived, even in those most primitive days. Their out-of-door existence was full of a wild charm, and their energy soon improved conditions indoors. Every ship from England brought over conveniences and luxuries. The cabin was exchanged for a substantial house. First pewter, and then silver plate began to shine on sideboards of polished oak. Four-post bedsteads decorated the sleeping rooms, and tapestry curtains kept out the cold.

A Maryland record of 1653 tells of a bargain between T. Wilford and Paul Sympson, by which, in consideration of twenty thousand pounds of tobacco received from Sympson, Wilford agrees to support him for the rest of his life "like a gentleman." This gentleman-like provision consisted of a house fifteen feet square, with a Welsh chimney, and lined with riven boards; a handsome joined bedstead, bedding and curtains; one small table, six stools, and three wainscot chairs; a servant to wait on him; meat, apparel, and washing; and every year an anker (ten gallons) of drams, one

THE COLONIAL CAVALIER.

tierce of sack, and a case of English spirits for his own use.

It is hard to imagine what more of luxury, an annuity could furnish to a gentleman of the nineteenth century, if indeed Heaven had blessed him with a stomach capable of consuming such an "intolerable deal of sack."

The next fifty years still further increased the elegance of living; and style as well as comfort began to be considered. In an inventory of household goods belonging to a Virginian in 1698, I find included, "a feather-bed, one sett Kitterminster curtains, and Vallens bedstead, one pair white linen sheets with two do. pillow biers, 2 Rusha-leather chaires, 5 Rush-bottom chaires, a burning glass, a flesk fork, and 6 Alchemy spoones" (alchemy being a mixed metal, originally supposed to be gold made by magic). In addition to these articles, the list includes a brass skimer and 2 pairs of pot-hooks, and, as its crowning glory, "1 old silver Dram-cup." No doubt the possessor had sat with his boon companions on many a cold night, by the great chimney, plunging the hot poker into the fire.—

"And nursed the loggerhead, whose hissing dip,
Timed by nice instinct, creamed the mug of flip."

The house of a planter in Virginia at the end of the seventeenth century, was substantial and comfortable. The inventory of such a planter mentions, as belonging to the homestead, a "parlor chamber, chamber over sd. chamber, chamber over the parlor, nursery, old nursery, room over the Ladyes chamber, Ladyes chamber, entry, store, home house quarter, home house, quarter over the creek, Smiths shopp, Barne, kitchen, Dary, chamber over the old Dary, flemings quarter, Robinsons quarter, Whitakers quarter, Black Wallnut Quarter."

By this time, the house of the rich in the towns boasted a parlor, but its furnishing was of the simplest. A white floor sprinkled with clean white sand, large tables, and heavy high-backed chairs of solid, dark oak decorated a parlor enough for anybody, says the chronicler of Baltimore. William Fitzhugh directs Mistress Sarah Bland in London (1682) to procure him a suit of tapestry hangings for a room twenty feet long, sixteen feet wide, and nine feet high; "and half a dozen chairs suitable."

The kitchen had long ago been separated from the dining-room, and, in the better houses, set off in a separate building, that its odours might not fill the other rooms when warm weather made open doors and windows necessary. The dining-room, with its broad buffet, its well-filled cellarette, its silver plate, and its quaint old English furniture, was generally the pleasantest room in the house. Opening out of the dining-room, between it and the parlor, ran the wide hall, with doors at either end, with carved stairway and panelled walls, often hung with family portraits.

Early in the eighteenth century, Spotswood came over as Governor of Virginia, and a new era of more elaborate living was introduced. His "palace" at Williamsburg, according to the contemporary report of the Reverend Hugh Jones—not to be taken, however, without a grain of salt—was "a magnificent structure, built at the publick expense, furnished and beautified with gates, fine gardens, offices, walks, a fine canal, orchards, etc.," and most impressive of all, in those days, when Sir Christopher Wren set the architectural fashions, "a cupola or lanthorn" illuminated on the King's birthnight, or other festival occasion. At Germanna, a little settlement of Germans clustered round the Spotswood iron-works, the Governor built him a house so fine that Colonel Byrd speaks of it as *The Enchanted Castle*, and has left an amusing account of a visit he made him there. "I arrived," he says, "about three o'clock, and found only Mrs. Spotswood at home. I was carried into a room elegantly set off with pier glasses, the largest of which came soon after to an odd misfortune. Amongst other favorite animals that cheered this lady's solitude, a brace of tame deer ran familiarly about the house, and one of them came to stare at me as a stranger. But unluckily, spying his own figure in the glass, he made a spring over the tea-table that stood under it and shattered the glass to pieces, and, falling back upon the tea-table, made a terrible fracas."

What a change is here, from the hewn timbers and bare walls and wooden trenchers of the pioneer, to enchanted castles and mirrors, and china and tea-tables!

This Colonel Byrd, who writes so genially of his visit to Germanna, was a typical cavalier—not godly, but manly—with a keen enjoyment of a jest, as the pucker at the corners of the lips in his portrait clearly shows, with a hearty good will toward his neighbor and especially his neighbor's wife, with a fine, healthy appetite, and a zest for all good things to eat and drink. In his boundary-line trip to Carolina and his journey to the mines, he smacks his lips over the fat things that fall in his way. Now it is a prime rasher of bacon, fricasseed in rum; now a capacious bowl of bombo. In one and the same paragraph, he tells how he commended his family to the care of the Almighty, fortified himself with a beefsteak, and kissed his landlady for good luck, before setting out on his travels.

THE COLONIAL CAVALIER.

Roughing it in camp, he dreams of the fine breakfast he will make on a fat doe, and a two-year-old bear, killed over night. At a stopping-place he records, "Our landlady cherished us with roast-beef and chicken-pie." Having eaten these with a relish, he pours down a basin of chocolate, wishes peace to that house, and takes up his line of march for home. There is something refreshing to our jaded generation in the hearty enjoyment that our ancestors took in their food.

I am struck in all these old gastronomic records with the immense amount of meat, in proportion to the vegetables used. No wonder gout was a common disease, and the overheated blood needed to be reduced by cupping and leeching. The out-of-door life, the riding and hunting of Maryland and Virginia, enabled the men to eat freely and drink deep, and the Southern table was always lavishly provided. A foreigner having remarked of Mrs. Madison that her table was like a Harvest-Home, she replied that, as the profusion which amused the visitor was the outgrowth of her country's prosperity, she was quite willing to sacrifice European elegance to Virginia liberality. Good housekeeping in those days consisted chiefly in setting a bountiful table, and the Colonial dame, in spite of her troop of servants, was kept busy in planning the meals, the breakfasts of hot bread and griddle-cakes, the afternoon dinner, and "the bite before bedtime." To her it fell, to carry the keys, to portion out the rations for the negro quarters, and to lay aside the materials from which the turbanned queen of the kitchen should compound the savory sausage, the fried chicken, the sauces, and dumplings, and cakes, which have made Southern cooking famous.

The domestic life of women on those old plantations must have been rather monotonous. The travellers who visited them, describe them as sharing little in the amusements of their husbands, and brothers, and sons. Chastellux says that, like the English, they are very fond of their *infants*, but care little for their *children;* but the annals and biographies do not bear out his statement. George Wythe learned his Greek at home, from a Testament, while his mother held an English copy in her hand and prompted him as he went on. John Mason, too, bore through life the impress of his mother's influence. He was only seven years old when she died, yet through life, "mother's room" was perfectly distinct to him, the old chest of drawers distinguished as *gown* drawer, *shirt* drawer, and *jacket* drawer, the closet known as mistress' closet, containing his mother's dresses, and another cupboard, known as *the* closet, in which hung a small green horsewhip with a silver head, carried by Mrs. Mason when she rode, and on other occasions used for purposes of correction, so that the children nicknamed it "the green doctor." An old letter recalls another "mother's room" in those eighteenth-century days: "On one side sits the chambermaid with her knitting; on the other a little colored pet, learning to sew. An old decent woman is there, with her table and shears, cutting out the negroes' winter clothes, while the old lady directs them all, incessantly knitting."

Home, rather than Church, was the sacred spot to the Colonial Cavalier, in spite of his theoretical reverence for Mother Church. It was at home that most of the baptisms and funerals occurred, and Hugh Jones complains that "in houses also they most commonly marry, without regard to the time of the day, or season of the year." The central idea of the Puritan religion was fear of God; the centre of the Cavalier's religion was love of man. From this root sprung a radiant cheerfulness, an open-handed liberality, and an unbounded hospitality. If it be true that the best ornaments of a house are its guests, never were houses more brilliantly decorated than those Southern mansions. The names of Brandon, and Berkeley, and Westover, and Mont Clare, and Doughoregan call up the procession of guests who have walked, and danced, and dined, and slept under their roofs.

THE COLONIAL CAVALIER.

We see stately men, in lace and ruffles, pacing the minuet with powdered dames, in "teacup time of hood and hoop, and when the patch was worn." We see lovers and maidens, brides and bridegrooms spending the honeymoon under the sheltering trees, and patriot Continentals arming in their halls for the struggle with the enemies of their country.

Not the lofty alone, but the lowly as well, could claim a welcome at those always open doors. Indians, half-breeds, and leather-clad huntsmen hung round the kitchen of Greenaway Court, while Washington and Lord Fairfax dined in the saloon. Not even acquaintance was considered necessary to ensure a cordial reception. "The inhabitants," wrote Beverly, "are very courteous to travellers, who need no other recommendation than being human creatures. A stranger has no more to do but to inquire upon the road where any gentleman or good housekeeper lives, and there he may depend upon being received with hospitality. This good-nature is so general among their people, that the gentry, when they go abroad, order their principal servants to entertain all visitors with everything the plantation affords; and the poor planters who have but one bed, will often sit up, or lie upon a form, or couch, all night, to make room for a weary traveller to repose himself after his journey."

THE COLONIAL CAVALIER.

In Winter, the fire blazed high on the hearth, and the toddy hissed in the noggin; in Summer, the basket of fruit stood in the breeze-swept hall, and lightly clad black boys tripped in, bearing cool tankards of punch and sangaree. The guest need only enter in, to be at home. No one was considered so contemptible, as he who consented to receive money for entertaining visitors. Keeping an inn or "ordinary" was looked upon askance, and the law dealt with the proprietor rigorously, as with one who probably would cheat if he got a chance. His charges were carefully regulated, and he was subject to fine, and even imprisonment, if he went beyond them. A Maryland statute provides that "noe Ordinary-Keeper within this Province shall at any Time charge anything to account for Boles of Punch, but shall only Sell the Severall Ingredients to the Said Mixture according to the Rates before in this Act Ascertained." A traveller, in those good old days, might ride from Maryland to Georgia, and never put up at an Ordinary at all, sure, whenever he wished to stop by the way, of a cordial welcome at a private house. Some planters even kept negroes posted at their gate, to give warning of a rider's approach, that he might be invited in, and that the household might be in readiness to receive him.

Such promiscuous hospitality could only exist

in a community with a happy faculty for taking life easily, an ability to dispense with the slavery to method, and to be contented though things went wrong. The fastidious European found some of the manners and customs a little trying. "In private houses as well as inns," writes a traveller, "several people are crowded together in the same room; and in the latter it very commonly happens that after you have been some time in bed, a stranger of any condition comes into the room, pulls off his clothes, and places himself without ceremony between your sheets."

Another visitor says that the Virginia houses are spacious, but the apartments are not commodious, "and they make no ceremony of putting three or four persons into the same room, nor do these make any objections to being thus heaped together."

The Colonial Cavalier was gregarious by nature. He was warmly social, and, being so much shut off by plantation life from intercourse with his fellows, he welcomed a guest as a special providence, to relieve the monotony of his life. The gentleman-planter in affluent circumstances had nothing to do, and he did it in a very leisurely way. His occupations were such as could be shared by a guest. An observant traveller has left us a vivid picture of the daily routine of such an individual:

THE COLONIAL CAVALIER.

"He rises about nine o'clock. He may perhaps make an excursion to walk as far as his stable to see his horses, which is seldom more than fifty yards from his house. He returns to breakfast between nine and ten, which is generally tea or coffee, bread and butter, and very thin slices of venison, ham, or hung beef. He then lies down on a pallet on the floor in the coolest room in the house, in his shirt and trousers only, with a negro at his head, and another to fan him and keep off the flies. Between twelve and one, he takes a draught of toddy or bombo, a liquor composed of water, sugar, rum and nutmeg, which is made weak, and kept cool. He dines between two and three, and at every table, whatever else there may be, a ham and greens, or cabbage, is always a standing dish. At dinner he drinks cider, toddy, punch, port, claret, and Madeira, which is generally excellent here. Having drunk some few glasses of wine after dinner, he returns to his pallet, with his two blacks to fan him, and continues to drink toddy or sangaree all the afternoon. He does not always drink tea. Between nine and ten in the evening, he eats a light supper of milk and fruit or wine, sugar and fruit, etc., and almost immediately retires to bed for the night."

All this sounds as if Smyth must have made his visit to Virginia in midsummer, and fancied that the habits were the same all the year round, as in that semi-tropical season. As a picture, it is truer of Carolina than of any section farther North. As we go South we find the character more indolent, the energies more relaxed, and even the houses changing their expression. The stately brick manor-houses, modelled on the English mansion, with their deep mullioned windows and heavy doors, give place to Italian villas, with white pillars and porches gleaming from their green points of land up and down the rivers. Under this shady porch the planter might lie at his ease, watching the boats on the streams as they come and go, and breathing the perfume from the garden at his feet. The garden of those days was laid out also on the Italian pattern, in shapes of horseshoes, or stars, or palm-leaves, with avenues leading down bordered by tulips trees, with box-hedged paths, wherein Corydon and Phyllis might wander, quite hidden from the lounger on the portico. In its centre stood often a summer-house, where successive generations plighted troth, and exchanged love-tokens. Everything about the garden, as about the house, suggested England. The lawn was sown with the seed of the silvery grass, so familiar in the great English parks. Even birds were imported from the mother country. When Spotswood came over, he brought with him a number of larks to delight his ears with their familiar strain, but either the climate was unpropitious, or the stronger native birds resented the coming of the foreigners, for the larks died out, and left only here and there a lonely descendant to startle the traveller as he rode along the solitary forest roads at sunrise, with a flow of melody that called up the leafy lanes of the old home.

Sweethearts and Wives

SWEETEHEARTS and WIVES

THE first settlers in America had no homes, for the first requisite for a home is a wife. They soon learned that "a better half, alone, gives better quarters." The Indian squaws were almost the only women known to the voyagers on the *Susan Constant* and her sister ships; and though the adventurers wrote home in glowing terms of their dusky charms, they looked askance upon the idea of marriage with the heathen natives. We cannot help, however, echoing the sentiments of Colonel Byrd of Westover, when he says: "Morals and all considered, I can't think the Indians much greater heathens than the first adventurers," who, he adds, "had they been good Christians, would have had the charity to take this only method of converting the natives to Christianity. For, after all that can be said, a sprightly lover is the most prevailing missionary that can be sent amongst these, or any other infidels. Besides," he proceeds candidly, "the poor Indians would have had less reason to complain that the English took away their lands, if they had received them by way of portion with their daughters."

It was, in truth, a great benefit both to the English and to the Indians, when "Bright-Stream-Between-two-Hills"—called in the native dialect "Pocahontas"—married John Rolfe, with the approbation of both races. To this union some of the proudest families in Virginia trace their descent. Poor little Princess! The first romance of America casts its pathetic charm around you. However apocryphal the legend of your saving Smith's life, it is hard to resist the impression of your cherishing a sentimental attachment for the gallant captain, and a suspicion that you were tricked into a marriage with Rolfe.

Smith records a sad interview with Pocahontas when she was being lionized, under the name of Lady Rebecca, as a royal visitor in London. "Being about this time preparing to set sail for New England," he writes, "I could not stay to do her that service I desired, and she well deserved; but, hearing she was at Bradford with divers of my friends, I went to see her. After a modest salutation without any bow, she turned about, obscured her face as not seeming well contented. But not long after, she began to talk, and remembered me well what courtesies she had done, saying: 'You did promise Powhatan what was yours should be his, and he the like to you; you called him Father—being in his land a stranger—and by the same reason so must I doe you.'" Smith objects on the ground of her royal lineage, which had well-nigh brought Rolfe to grief, and she responds: "Were you not afraid to come into my father's countrie and cause feare in him and all his people but mee, and feare you here I should call you Father? I tell you then I will; and you shall call me childe; and soe will I be forever and ever your countrieman. They did tell me always you were dead, and I knew no other till I came to Plymouth. Yet Powhatan did command Ottamatomakkin to seek you and know the truth, because your countriemen will lie much." So ended the parting; and soon afterward the poor little Princess died a stranger in a strange land. "She came to Gravesend, to her end and grave."

The first English wedding on American soil was solemnized between John Laydon, a laborer, and

THE COLONIAL CAVALIER.

Anne Buras, maid to Mistress Forest. They were "marry'd together" in 1608. Eleven years later came a ship bearing "ye maides," a company of ninety young women, "pure and uncorrupt," sent over to Virginia, at the expense of the company in London, to be married to such settlers as were able and willing to support them, and to refund to the company the cost of passage. A little later, sixty more "maides" followed; and though the cost of a wife rose from a hundred and twenty, to a hundred and fifty pounds of tobacco, there was no slackening in the demand. In Maryland, as late as 1660, the market was equally brisk. "The first planters," says the record, "were so far from expecting money with a woman, that 'twas a common thing for them to buy a deserving wife, that carried good testimonials of her character, at the price of a hundred pound, and make themselves believe they had a bargain."

We read of an adventurous young lady of some social consequence, being a niece of Daniel Defoe, who, suffering from an unfortunate love-affair in England, ran away from home, and came to Maryland as a "redemptioner." Her services were engaged by a farmer named Job, in Cecil County, and soon after, according to a frequent custom of the country, she married into the family of her employer. A Maryland record of November 2, 1638, runs thus: "This day came William Lewis, planter, and made oath that he is not recontracted to any other woman than Ursula Gifford; and that there is no impediment why he should not be married to the said Ursula Gifford—and, further, he acknowledgeth himself to owe unto the Lord Proprietary a thousand pounds of tobacco, in case there be any precontract or other lawful impediment whatsoever, as aforesaid, either on the part of William Lewis or Ursula Gifford."

This arrangement of making the bridegroom responsible for the good faith of the lady as well as his own, is quite refreshing in these days of equal rights and responsibilities. The woman's rights question, however, was at the front in Maryland, in the seventeenth century; and the strong-minded woman who introduced it, was Mistress Margaret Brent, cousin to Governor Calvert, who had such confidence in her business sagacity and ability, that he appointed her his executrix, with the brief instructions, "Take all: pay all." She made application to the Maryland Assembly to grant her a vote in the House for herself, and another as his Lordship's attorney. The request was peremptorily refused by Governor Greene; but, nothing daunted, "the sd. Mrs Brent protested against all proceedings in this present assembly unlesse shee may be present and have a vote as aforesaid."

THE COLONIAL CAVALIER.

Another woman of force in those days was Virlinda Stone. In the Maryland archives still exists a letter from her to Lord Baltimore, praying for an investigation of a fight in Anne Arundel County, during which her husband was wounded. At the end of the business-like document, she adds a fiery and altogether feminine postscript, in which she declares that "Hemans, the master of the *Golden Lion*, is a very knave: and that will be made plainly for to appeare to your Lordship, for he hath abused my husband most grossly." Such women as these were not to be trifled with. No wonder Alsop says: "All complimental courtships drest up in critical Rarities are meer strangers to them. Plain wit comes nearest to their genius; so that he that intends to court a Maryland girle, must have something more than the tautologies of a long-winded speech to carry on his design, or else he may fall under the contempt of her frown and his own windy discourse."

The Virginia women were as high-spirited as their Maryland sisters. They had no idea of being commanded into matrimony. When Governor Nicholson became infatuated with one of the fair daughters of Master Lewis Burwell and demanded her hand with royally autocratic manner, neither she nor her parents were disposed to comply. The suitor became furious, and persisted for years in his determination, which seems to have been as much a matter of pride, as of sentiment. He took pains to wreak his wrath on every one who opposed the match, going so far as to threaten the lives of the unwilling young woman's father and brother. To Commissary Blair he declared that, if she married any one but himself, he would cut the throats of three men—the bridegroom, the minister, and the justice who issued the license. Strangely enough, the damsel was not attracted by this wild wooing; and, as a candid friend wrote to the furious lover, "It is not here, as in some barbarous countries, where the tender lady is dragged into the Sultan's arms reeking with the blood of her relatives." Though this affair created such a stir throughout the Colony of Virginia and lasted so long a time, no record has remained of the young heroine's after fate, except the fact that she did not become Lady Nicholson; not even her Christian name has come down to posterity, to whom she remains a shadowy divinity.

A noticeable feature of Colonial life in Virginia, is the belleship of widows. The girls seem to have stood no chance against their fascinations. Washington, and Jefferson, and Madison each married one. In the preceding century, Sir William Berkeley, who had brought no lady with him across the water, was taken captive by a young widow of Warwick County, a certain Dame Frances Stevens, who, after thirty-two years of married life, being again left a widow by Berkeley's death, wedded with her late husband's secretary, Philip Ludwell —holding fast, however, to her title of Lady Berkeley. Lord Culpeper writes in a letter of 1680, "My Lady Berkeley is married to Mr. Ludwell; and thinks no more of our world." It is to be hoped that the secretary whom the lady took for her third husband, proved a more amiable companion than the fiery old Governor, whose pride and bitter obstinacy wrought such havoc after Bacon's rebellion, that the reports of his cruelties echoed to the shores of England. Edmund Cheesman, a follower of Bacon's, being brought up for trial, Berkeley asked him: "Why did you engage in Bacon's designs?" Before Cheesman could answer, his young wife, falling on her knees, exclaimed: "My provocation made my husband join in the cause for which Bacon contended. But for me he had never done what he has done. Let me bear the punishment, but let my husband be pardoned!" Where was the chivalry of that Cavalier blood on which Berkeley prided himself? We read that her prayer availed her husband nothing, and procured only insult to herself.

Our sympathy with Bacon, in his rebellion

against Berkeley's tyranny, makes us doubly regretful that he should have stained his career by a deed of cowardice and cruelty. It was one of those blunders worse than crimes, and gave him and his followers the contemptuous appellation of "White Aprons." When Bacon made his sudden turn on Sir William Berkeley, he established his headquarters at *Green Spring*, Berkeley's own mansion. There he threw up breastworks in front of his palisades, and then sent out detachments of horsemen, who scoured the country and brought back to camp the wives of prominent Berkeleyites. Among these dames were Madam Bray, Madam Page, Madam Ballard, and Madam Bacon—the last, the wife of the rebel's kinsman. Bacon then sent one of the dames to the town under a flag of truce, to inform the husbands that he intended to place them in front of his men while he constructed his earthworks. "The poor gentlewomen were mightily astonished, and neather were their husbands void of amazement at this subtile invention. The husbands thought it indeed wonderful that their innocent and harmless wives should thus be entered a white garde to the Divell"—the *Divell*, of course, being General Bacon, who, thus protected by *The White Aprons*, finished his fortifications in security; gaining a reputation for "subtility," but tarnishing his character for gallantry.

THE COLONIAL CAVALIER.

As society grew more stable, it grew also more complex. The buying of wives gave way to sentimental courtships, and men also began to learn the advantages of a single life. In Maryland so many took this view, that we find the old statutes imposing a tax on bachelors over twenty-five years of age, of five shillings, for estates under three hundred pounds sterling, or twenty shillings when over; a tax which seems to have been more successful as a means of raising money than of promoting matrimony; for we find the record of its payment by a surprising number of bachelors, St. Ann's parish vestry-books alone showing thirty-four such derelicts. Perhaps, however, this celibacy did not indicate so much aversion to marriage, as inability to meet the growing demands for luxury. The obstinate bachelors may have felt with regard to matrimony as Alsop did with regard to liberty, that "without money it is like a man opprest with the gout—every step he takes forward puts him to pain." The Abbé Robin at a later day says of Annapolis: "Female luxury here exceeds what is known in the provinces of France. A French hair-dresser is a man of importance; it is said a certain dame here, hires one of that craft at a thousand crowns a year salary." The very rumors of such extravagance must have frightened frugal young men!

THE COLONIAL CAVALIER.

The Colonial maiden came into society and married, at an age which now seems surprisingly early. Chief-Justice Marshall met and fell in love with his wife when she was fourteen, and married her at sixteen. An unmarried woman of over twenty-five, was looked upon as a hopeless and confirmed old maid and spoken of, like Miss Wilkins, of Boston, as "a pitiable spectacle." It may be that this extreme youth of the maids explains the attraction of the widows, who had more social experience. Burnaby writes in a very unhandsome manner of his impressions of the Virginia ladies whom he met in his American tour, and generalizes with true British freedom on slight acquaintance with the facts. He admits grudgingly that the women of Virginia are handsome, "though not to be compared with our fair countrywomen in England. They have but few advantages, and consequently are seldom accomplished. This makes them reserved and unequal to any interesting or refined conversation. They are immoderately fond of dancing, and, indeed, it is almost the only amusement they partake of; but even in this, they discover great want of taste and elegance, and seldom appear with that gracefulness and ease which these movements are so calculated to display. Toward the close of an evening, when the company are pretty well tired with contra-dances, it is usual to dance jigs—a practice originally borrowed, I am informed, from the negroes. The Virginia ladies, excepting these amusements, and now and then a party of pleasure into the woods to partake of a barbecue, cheerfully spend their time in sewing and taking care of their families."

Another traveller makes a better report, and draws more favorable conclusions.

"Young women are affable with young men in America," he writes, "and married women are reserved, and their husbands are not as familiar with the girls as they were, when bachelors. If a young man were to take it into his head that his betrothed should not be free and gay in her social intercourse, he would run the risk of being discarded, incur the reputation of jealousy, and would find it very difficult to get married. Yet if a single woman were to play the coquette, she would be regarded with contempt. As this innocent freedom between the sexes diminishes in proportion as society loses its purity and simplicity of manners, as is the case in cities, I desire sincerely that our good Virginia ladies may long retain their liberty entire."

The Colonial age was the day of elaborate compliment. Gentlemen took time to turn their sentences and polish them neatly, and ladies heard them to the end without suggesting by a word or glance that the climax had been foreseen for the last five minutes, at least. An essay on *Woman*, by a certain Mr. Thomas, had a great vogue in the eighteenth century, and antedated Tupper's Poems as a well of sentimental quotation. *The Spectator* and *The Tattler* gave the tone to society literature, and enabled the provincial dame to reflect accurately the Lady Betty Modish of London. The beaux, too, took many a leaf from *The Spectator* in the study of a compliment. When I read of the Colonial maiden poring over the tiny glaze-paper note accompanying a book entitled "The Art of Loving"—in which the writer declares it to be "most convenient, presenting the *art of Loving* to one who so fully possesses the *art of Pleasing*"—I am carried back to the days of Sir Charles Grandison.

There is a marked contrast in the social chronicles of the eighteenth century at home and abroad, between what the gentlemen said *to* the ladies and what they said *about* them. That wicked Colonel Byrd, for instance, after making himself agreeable to Governor Spotswood's ladies the whole evening, writes in his journal that their conversation was "like whip sillabub—very pretty, but with nothing in it." Again he describes himself patronizingly as "prattling with the ladies after a nine o'clock supper." Yet, underneath all the superficial bowing and scraping of courtesy and compliment, and the jesting asides at the expense of the fair sex, it must be set down to the Cavalier's credit that he treated womankind with a great tenderness and respect. Woman's influence made itself felt in private and in public—in the Council, in the Virginia House of Burgesses, and in the Assemblies of Maryland and of Carolina.

The pride and folly of Governor Tryon of Carolina led him to make a demand on the Assembly for an extensive appropriation for the building of a palace at Newbern suitable for the residence of a royal Governor. To obtain this appropriation, Lady Tryon and her sister, the beautiful Esther Wake, used all their blandishments. Lady Tryon gave brilliant balls and dinners, and her sister's bright eyes rained influence to such good purpose, that the first appropriation and as much more was granted, and the palace was pronounced the most magnificent structure in America. The palace is fallen—its marble mantels, its colonnades, its carved staircases are in ruins; but the name of beautiful Esther Wake is preserved in Wake County.

The chronicles of the Carolinas are full of romance. Here, at Cross Creek, dwelt Flora Mac-

THE COLONIAL CAVALIER.

Donald, the heroic rescuer of the Pretender after the disasters of Culloden. It seems a strange chance that brought her from such exciting masquerades, from the companionship of kings and the rôle of heroine on the stage of the great world, to the pioneer's cottage in the wild woods of the Western wilderness. The only drawback to her career in eighteenth century eyes was that she married and lived happy ever after. The romance of that day demanded a broken heart, and tragedy was always in high favor. Every locality had its story of blighted love and life. The Dismal Swamp, lying on the border between Virginia and Maryland, was a sort of Gretna Green, where many runaway marriages were celebrated. Tradition tells of a lover whose sweetheart died suddenly; and he, driven mad by grief, fancied that she had gone to the Dismal Swamp, where he perished in the search for her.

When Tom Moore was in this country he was impressed by the legend, and set it thus to the music—let us not dare to say the jingle—of his verse:

> They made her a grave too cold and damp
>   For a soul so warm and true,
> And she's gone to the Lake of the Dismal Swamp,
> Where all night long, by her fire-fly lamp
>   She paddles her white canoe.

THE COLONIAL CAVALIER.

And her fire-fly lamp I soon shall see,
  Her paddle I soon shall hear.
Long and loving our life shall be,
And I'll hide the maid in a cypress tree,
  When the footsteps of Death draw near.

Real life had its tragedies, too. In the deep wainscoted hall of the Brandon Mansion hangs a portrait of lovely Evelyn Byrd. She sits on a green bank, with a handful of roses and a shepherd's crook in her lap—her soft, dark eyes look out in pensive sadness as though they could, if they would, tell the story of a maiden's heart and a life ended untimely by unhappy love. One story says she broke her heart for Parke Custis, who left her to wear the willow, and married afterward the Martha Dandridge, who in the whirligig of time became Lady Washington. Another rumor connects her name with that of the Earl of Peterborough, who loved her deeply, so the story runs; but his creed was not hers, and her father, Colonel Byrd, would not consent to the marriage. The maiden yielded to her father's will, but pined away and died; and there, in the Westover burying-ground, she lies under a ponderous stone, which records this epitaph:

> "Alas, Reader,
> We can detain nothing, however valued,
> From unrelenting death,
> Beauty, Fortune, or exalted Honour—
> See here a proof!"

"Brandon," James River, Va.

I cannot help feeling that all these might have been detained on earth to a ripe age, had the maiden been left free to decide the most important question of her life to her liking; for, in a letter written by Colonel Byrd when Evelyn was a slip of a girl, I read concerning the maiden, "She has grown a great romp and enjoys robust health." Yet a few years later, the robust romp has faded to a shadow, and is laid away in the family graveyard, and only her portrait by Sir Godfrey Kneller, remains to appeal to the sentiment and sympathy of posterity.

The gentle Evelyn Byrd was not the only one whom the traditions of the Colonial Cavalier credit with carrying to the grave a heart scarred with the wounds of unhappy love. Lord Fairfax, who lived to be over sixty and kept open house at Belvoir, where Washington visited him and kept him company in riding to hounds over hill and dale; Lord Fairfax—with his gaunt, tall frame; his gray, nearsighted eyes, and prominent aquiline nose, little outward resemblance as he might bear to the original of the almond-eyed portrait at Brandon—resembled her at least in a wounded heart and a broken career. In his youth, this solitary Virginia recluse had been a brilliant man-about-town in the gay world of London. He had held a commission in "the Blues"; he had known the famous men of the day, he had dabbled in literature, and contributed a paper now and then to the *Spectator*. When his career of fashion was at its height, he paid his addresses to a young lady of rank and was accepted. The day for the wedding was fixed—the establishment furnished, even to equipage and servants—when the inconstant bride-elect, dazzled by a ducal coronet, broke her engagement. The blow wrought a complete change in the jilted lover. From that time he shrank from the society of all women, and finally came over to Virginia to hide his hurt in the Western forests.

Spite of such traditions of melancholy, the actual career of most of the people of those times forms a curious contrast to the ideals of their poetry and fiction. With scarcely an exception, they survived their unsuccessful love affairs, and lived in prosperous serenity with others than the first rulers of their hearts.

There is Jefferson, for instance. Almost the first letter in his published correspondence is devoted to a confession of his tender passion for a young lady dwelling in the town of Williamsburg. Yet her name is not the one that stands next his own on the marriage register. This first love of his was a Miss 'Becca Burwell. We chance upon the young collegian's secret as we open his letter to John Page, written on Christmas day, 1762. He begins jocularly enough, yet only half in fun after all: "I am sure if there is such a thing as a Devil in this world, he must have been here last night, and have had some hand in contriving what happened to me. Do you think the cursed rats (at his instigation, I suppose) did not eat up my pocket-book, which was in my pocket, within a foot of my head? And not contented with plenty for the present, they carried away my jemmy-worked silk garters and half a dozen new minuets I had just got." "Tell Miss Alice Corbin," he adds, "that I verily believe the rats knew I was to win a pair of garters from her, or they never would have been so cruel as to carry mine away."

Christmas day, indeed, found him in sorry case. These losses he could have borne, but worse remained to tell: "You know it rained last night, or if you do not know it, I am sure I do. When I went to bed I laid my watch in the usual place; and going to take her up after I arose this morning, I found her in the same place, 'tis true, but— *quantum mutatus ab illo*—all afloat in water, let in at a leak in the roof of the house, and as silent and still as the rats that had eat my pocket-book. Now, you know, if chance had had anything to do in this matter, there were a thousand other spots where it might have chanced to leak as well as this one, which was perpendicularly over my watch. But, I'll tell you, it's my opinion that the Devil came and bored the hole over it on purpose." It was not the injury to his timepiece which drew forth these violent, half-real, half-jesting objurgations; no, there was a sentimental reason behind. The water had soaked a watch-paper and a picture, so that when he attempted to remove them, he says: "My cursed fingers gave them such a rent as I fear I shall never get over. I would have cried bitterly, but that I thought it beneath the dignity of a man!" The mystery of the original of the picture and the maker of the watch-paper is soon explained, for a page or two further on, he trusts that Miss 'Becca Burwell will give him another watch-paper of her own cutting, which he promises to esteem much more, though it were a plain round one, than the nicest in the world cut by other hands. "However," he adds, "I am afraid she would think this presumption, after my suffering the other to get spoiled."

A very real and tumultuous passion this of young Tom Jefferson's! Every letter he writes to his friend teems with reference to *her*. Now she is R. B.; again Belinda; and again, with that deep secrecy of dog Latin so dear to the collegian, she figures as *Campana in die* (bell in day); or, still more mysteriously, as Adnileb, written in Greek that the vulgar world may not pry into the sacred secret. Oh, youth, youth, how like is the nineteenth century to the eighteenth, and that to its preceding, till we reach the courtship of Adam and Eve!

In October, '63, he writes to his old confidant: "In the most melancholy fit that ever any poor soul was, I sit down to write you. Last night, as merry as agreeable company and dancing with Belinda in the Apollo could make me, I never could have thought the succeeding sun could have seen me so wretched as I now am! . . . I was prepared to say a great deal. I had dressed up in my own mind such thoughts as occurred to me in as moving a language as I knew how, and expected to have performed in a tolerably creditable manner. But, good God! when I had an opportunity of venting them, a few broken sentences, uttered in great disorder and interrupted with pauses of uncommon length, were the too visible marks of my strange confusion." The framer of the Declaration of Independence, whose eloquence startled the world, found himself tongue-tied and stammering in a declaration of love to a provincial maiden.

At twenty-nine or thirty Jefferson had recovered enough to go a-courting again, to Mistress Martha Skelton, a young and childless widow, of

THE COLONIAL CAVALIER

such great beauty that many rivals contested with him the honor of winning her hand. The story goes that two of these rivals met one evening in Mrs. Skelton's drawing-room. While waiting for her to enter, they heard her singing in an adjoining room, to the accompaniment of Jefferson's violin. The love-song was so expressively executed that the admirers perceived that their doom was sealed, and, picking up their cocked hats, they stole out without waiting for the lady.

If Jefferson in his younger days was soft-hearted toward the gentler sex, his susceptibility was as nothing compared to Washington's. The sentimental biography of that great man would be more entertaining than the story of his battles, or his triumphs of government. There are evidences in his own handwriting that, before he was fifteen years old, he had conceived a passion for a fair unknown beauty, so serious as to disturb his otherwise well-regulated mind, and make him seriously unhappy. His sentimental poems written at that age, are neither better nor worse than the productions of most boys of fifteen. One of them hints that bashfulness has prevented his divulging his passion:

> "Ah, woe is me, that I should love and conceal!
> Long have I wished and never dare reveal."

At the mature age of sixteen, he writes to his "dear friend Robin": "my residence is at present at his Lordship's, where I might, *was my heart disengaged,* pass my time very pleasantly, as there's a very agreeable young lady lives in the same house; but as that's only adding fuel to the fire, it makes me the more uneasy; for by often and unavoidably (!) being in company with her, revives my former passion for your Lowland Beauty; whereas, was I to live more retired from young women, I might in some measure alleviate my sorrows by burying that chaste and troublesome passion in the grave of oblivion." This "chaste and troublesome passion" had subsided enough, when he went as a young officer to New York in all the gorgeousness of uniform and trappings, to enable him to fall in love with Miss Mary Phillipse, whom he met at the house of her sister, Mrs. Beverly Robinson. She was gay, she was rich, she was beautiful, and Washington might have made her the offer of his heart and hand; but suddenly an express from Winchester brought word to New York of a French and Indian raid, and young Washington hastened to rejoin his command, leaving the capture of the lady to Captain Morris. Three years later we find him married to the Widow Custis, with two children and a fortune of fifteen thousand pounds sterling. Shortly after, he writes of himself from Mount Vernon, temperately enough, as "fixed in this seat with an agreeable partner for life," and we hear no more of amatory verses in honor of his Lowland Beauty, or flirtations with fashionable young dames in New York. But when the Marquis de Chastellux announced his marriage, Washington wrote him in a vein of humor rather foreign to him, and bespeaking a genial sympathy in his expectations of happiness. "I saw by the eulogium you often made on the happiness of domestic life in America," he writes, "that you had swallowed the bait, and that you would as surely be taken one day or other, as that you were a philosopher and a soldier. So your day has at length come! I am glad of it with all my heart and soul. It is quite good enough for you. Now you are well served for coming to fight in favor of the American rebels all the way across the Atlantic Ocean, by catching that terrible contagion—domestic felicity—which, like the small-pox or plague, a man can have only once in his life."

Of all the joyous festivals among the Southern Colonists, none was so mirthful as a wedding. The early records of the wreck of the Sea Venture and the tedious and dangerous delay on the Bermudas mention that in even that troublous time they held one "merry English wedding." In any

THE COLONIAL CAVALIER.

new land marriages and births are joyful events. All that is needed for prosperity is multiplication of settlers, and so it is quite natural that the setting up of a new household should be celebrated with rejoicing and merry-making.

In one respect the colonists broke with the home traditions. They insisted on holding their marriage ceremonies at home rather than in church, and no minister could move their determination. As civilization advanced, and habits grew more luxurious, the marriage festivities grew more elaborate and formal. The primitive customs gave way to pomp and display, till at length a wedding became an affair of serious expense. "The house of the parents," says Scharf in his "Chronicles of Baltimore," "would be filled with company to dine; the same company would stay to supper. For two days punch was dealt out in profusion. The gentlemen saw the groom on the first floor, and then ascended to the second floor, where they saw the bride; there every gentleman, even to one hundred a day, kissed her."

A Virginia wedding in the olden time was a charming picture—the dancers making merry in the wide halls or on the lawn; the black servants dressed in fine raiment for the occasion and showing their white teeth in that enjoyment only possible to a negro; the jolly parson acting at once as priest and toast-master; the groom in ruffles and velvet, and the bride in brocade and jewels. Never again will our country have so picturesque a scene to offer. Let us recall it while we may!

His Dress

His Dress

"In teacup time of hood and hoop
And when the patch was worn"

IF you have any curiosity to know what clothes these first Colonial Cavaliers wore, you may learn very easily by reading over the "particular of Apparrell" upon which they agreed as necessary to the settler bound for Virginia.

The list includes: "1 dozen Points, a Monmouth cap, 1 waste-coat, 3 falling bands, 1 suit of canvase, 3 shirts, 1 suit of frieze, 1 suit of cloth, 4 paire shoes, 3 paire Irish stockings, and 1 paire garters." Besides these he would need "1 Armor compleat, light, a long peece, a sword, a belt and a Bandelier," which may be reckoned among his wearing apparel, for it would be long before the settler could be safe without them when he ventured outside the palisade.

Englishmen in those days were fond of elaborate dress. It was the period of conical hats, and rosetted shoes, of doublets and sashes and padded trunk-hose, which his Majesty, James the First, much affected because they filled out his ill-shaped legs. Suits of clothes were a frequent form of gift and bequest. Captain John Smith's will declares, "I give unto Thomas Packer, my best suite of aparrell, of a tawney colour, viz., hose, doublet, jerkin and cloake."

The peruke began its all-conquering career in England, under the Stuarts. Elizabeth, it is true, had owned eighty suits of hair, and Mary of Scotland had varied her hair to match her dresses. But a defect of the French Dauphin introduced the use of the wig for men as well as women, and false hair became the rage throughout the world of fashion. A London peruke-maker advertised: "Full-bottom wigs, full bobs, minister's bobs, naturals, half-naturals, Grecian flyes, Curleyroys, airey levants, qu perukes and baggwiggs." The customer must have been hard to please, who could find nothing to suit his style in such a stock.

The settlers in Colonial America did not allow themselves such luxuries of the toilet as a variety of wigs, though a well-planned peruke or "a bob" might have been a good device to trick the tomahawk of the savage into a bloodless scalping. With the poorer people, a single wig for Sunday wear sufficed, and was replaced on week days by a cap, generally of linen.

The Colonial dames, being too far from Court to

copy the low-necked dresses, the stomachers and farthingales of the inner circle of fashion, wore instead, huge ruffs, full, short petticoats, and long, flowing sleeves, over tight undersleeves. Even in the wilderness, however, they retained a feminine fondness for gay attire.

John Pory, a clever scapegrace intimately acquainted with gaming-tables and sponging-houses in London, but figuring in Virginia as secretary to Governor Yeardley, wrote home to Sir Dudley Carleton, "That your Lordship may know that we are not the veriest beggars in the world, our cowkeeper here of James Cittie, on Sundays goes accoutred all in fresh flaming silk, and a wife of one that in England professed the black art, not of a scholar but of a collier of Croydon, wears her rough beaver hat with a fair pearl hat-band and a silken suit, thereto correspondent."

Lively John was probably lying a little in the cause of immigration, but it is certain that the desire for fine clothes early called for a check, and at an early session of the Virginia House of Burgesses, a sumptuary law was passed "against excess in apparell," directing "that every man be ceffed in the church for all publique contributions—if he be unmarried, according to his own apparell; if he be married, according to his own and his wives, or either of their apparell."

Here, surely, is a suggestion from the past, for the fashionable church of the present.

A later law in the provinces enacts that "no silke stuffe in garments or in peeces, except for hoods or scarfes, nor silver or gold lace, nor bone-lace of silke or thread, nor ribbands wrought with silver or gold in them, shall be brought into this country to sell, after the first of February." A Maryland statute proposes that two sorts of "cloaths" only be worn, one for summer, the other for winter. But this was going too far, and the law was never enforced.

It was permitted to none but Members of the Council and Heads of Hundreds in Virginia to wear the coveted gold on their clothes, or to wear any silk not made by themselves. This last prohibition was intended not so much to discourage pomp and pride, as to stimulate the infant industry of silk production, which from the beginning had been a pet scheme of the colonists. They had imported silk-worms and planted mulberry trees; and as an inducement to go into the business, the Burgesses offered a premium of five thousand pounds of tobacco to any one making a hundred pounds of wound silk in any one year.

His Gracious Majesty, Charles the Second, sent to his loyal subjects in Virginia, a letter, still to be seen in the college library at Williamsburg. It is written by his Majesty's private secretary and signed with the sacred "Charles R." It is addressed to Governor Berkeley, and runs:

"Trusty & Wellbeloved, We Greet You Well. Wee have received wth much content ye dutifull respects of Our Colony in ye prefent lately made us by you & ye councell there, of ye firft product of ye new Manufacture of Silke, which as a mark of Our Princely acceptation of yor duteys & for y^r particular encouragement, etc.—Wee have commanded to be wrought up for ye ufe of Our owne perfon."

From this letter has sprung the legend, dear to loyalist hearts, that the robe worn by Charles at his coronation was woven of Virginia silk.

So much material was needed "for ye use of our owne person," that the offering of silk was no doubt very welcome. The King's favorite, Buckingham, had twenty-seven suits, one of them of white uncut velvet, set all over with diamonds and worn with diamond hat-bands, cockades and ear-rings, and yoked with ropes and knots of pearls.

It was an era of wild extravagance. Not satisfied with the elegance of the time of Charles First, his son's courtiers added plumes to the wide-brimmed hats, enlarged the bows on the shoes, donned great wigs, loaded their vests with embroidery, and over their coats hung short cloaks, worth a fortune.

The women dressed as befitted the court of a dissolute king. Their artificial curls were trained in "heart-breakers" and "love-locks." The whiteness of their skin was enhanced by powder and set off by patches. Their shoulders rose above bodices of costly brocade hung with jewels which had sometimes ruined both buyer and wearer.

The Puritans, by their opposition to the Court, escaped the evil influences of these extravagances. But the Colonial Cavaliers, who bowed before the King lower than the courtiers at home, of course imitated his dress, so far as their fortunes allowed. Every frigate that came into port at Jamestown or St. Maries brought the latest London fashions. A little before Colonel Fitzhugh in Virginia was ordering his Riding Camblet cloak from London, Mr. Samuel Pepys was writing in his journal, "This morning came home my fine camlete cloak with gold buttons." While this gentleman was attiring himself in his new shoulder-belt and tunique laced with silk, "and so very handsome to church," Sir William Berkeley and Governor Calvert were opening their eyes of a Sunday morning three thousand miles away, and making ready to get into their rosetted shoes, and to lace their breeches and hose together with points as fanciful

as his, and, like him, perhaps, having their heads "combed by y^e maide for *powder and other troubles.*" No doubt Lady Berkeley, in her fine lace bands, her coverchef and deep veil, was as fine as Madam Pepys in her paragon pettycoat and "*just a corps.*"

With the beginning of the eighteenth century, the hoop appeared, and carried all before it, in more senses than one. "The ladies' petticoats," I read in the notes of a contemporary of the fashion, "are now blown up into a most enormous concave." Over this concave the ladies wore, on ceremonious occasions, such as a ball at Governor Spotswood's or an assembly at Annapolis, trailing gowns of heavy brocade, many yards in length. Dragging these skirts behind, and bearing aloft on their heads a towering structure of feathers, ribbons and lace, it was no wonder these dames preferred slow and stately measures. At their side, or as near as the spreading hoop permitted, moved their favored cavaliers, their coat-skirts stiff with buckram, their swords dangling between their knees, their breeches of red plush or black satin, so tight that they fitted without a wrinkle.

Men of that day took their dress very seriously. Washington, who had doubtless gained many ideas of fashion from the modish young officers of Braddock's army, ordered his costumes with as much particularity as he afterward conducted his campaigns. Shortly before he started with his little cavalcade of negro servants on his five-hundred-mile ride to Massachusetts, in 1756, he sent over to a correspondent in London an order for an extensive wardrobe. He wanted "2 complete livery suits for servants, with a spare cloak and all other necessary trimmings for two suits more." He omits no detail. "I would have you," he writes, "choose the livery by our arms; only as the field is white, I think the clothes had better not be quite so, but nearly like the inclosed. The trimmings and facings of scarlet, and a scarlet waistcoat. If livery lace is not quite disused, I should be glad to have the cloaks laced. I like that fashion best, and two silver-laced hats for the above servants."

In addition to this, he wishes "1 set of horse-furniture with livery lace, with the Washington crest on the housings, etc. The cloak to be of the same piece and color of the clothes, 3 gold and scarlet sword-knots, 3 silver and blue ditto, 1 fashionable gold-laced hat."

It is not strange that the gallant young officer made a sensation among the dames and damsels of Philadelphia and New York as he journeyed northward, nor that Mistress Mary Phillipse nearly lost her heart to the wearer of the gold and scarlet sword-knots and the fashionable gold-laced hat.

All society went in gorgeous array in those gay

days, before color had been banished to suit the grim taste of the Puritan, and to meet the economical maxims of *Poor Richard.* Judges, on the bench, wore robes of scarlet, faced with black velvet, exchanged in summer for thinner ones of silk. Etiquette demanded equally formal costume for advocates at the bar. Patrick Henry, who began by indifference to dress, even rushing into court fresh from the chase, with mud and mire clinging to his leather breeches, at length yielded to social pressure, and donned a full suit of black velvet in which to address the court; and, on one occasion at least, a peach-colored coat effectively set off by a bag-wig, powdered, as pompous Mr. Wirt observes, "in the highest style of forensic fashion."

A satirical description sets forth the dress of a dandy in the middle of the eighteenth century, as consisting of "a coat of light green, with sleeves too small for the arms, and buttons too big for the sleeves; a pair of Manchester fine stuff breeches, without money in the pockets; clouded silk stockings, but no legs; a club of hair behind, larger than the head that carries it; a hat of the size of a sixpence, on a block not worth a farthing."

In October, 1763, the free-school at Annapolis was broken into by robbers, and the wardrobe of the master stolen. When I remember the scanty salaries paid to these schoolmasters, I look with surprise on the inventory, which the victim of the robbery publishes. Here we have a superfine blue broadcloth frock coat, a new superfine scarlet waistcoat bound with gold lace, a pair of green worsted breeches lined with dimity, besides a ruffled shirt, pumps, and doe-skin breeches. A very pretty wardrobe, I should say, for the teacher of a Colonial village-school!

It was a picturesque world in those days. The gentry rode gayly habited in bright-colored velvets and ruffles; the clergy swept along in dignified black; the judges wore their scarlet robes, and the mechanics and laborers were quite content to don a leather apron over their buckskin breeches and red-flannel jacket. The slaves in Carolina were forbidden to wear anything, except when in livery, finer than negro-cloth, duffils, kerseys, osnaburgs, blue linen, check-linen, coarse garlix or calicoes, checked cotton, or Scotch plaid. This prohibition was quite unnecessary, as the slave thought himself very lucky if he were clad in a new and whole garment of any sort.

Even paupers had their distinctive badges. A Virginia statute commands that every person who shall receive relief from the parish, and be sent to the poorhouse, shall, upon the shoulder of the right sleeve of his, or her, uppermost garment, in an open and visible manner, wear a badge with the name of the parish to which he, or she, belongs, cut either in blue, red, or green cloth, at the will of the vestry or churchwardens. If any unfortunate were afflicted with pride as well as poverty and refused to wear this badge of pauperism, he was subject, by the law, to a whipping, not to exceed five lashes.

The students of William and Mary College were required to wear academical dress as soon as they had passed "ye grammar school," and thus another costume was added to the moving tableaux on the street of Williamsburg.

In the college-books, I find it resolved by the Faculty in 1765 that Mrs. Foster be appointed stocking-mender in the college, and that she be paid annually the sum of £12, provided she furnishes herself with lodging, diet, fire, and candles. Considering the length of stockings in those days, and assuming that the nature of boys has not materially changed, I cannot help thinking the salary somewhat meagre for the duties involved. Stockings, however, were less troublesome than shirts. A Mrs. Campbell sends her nephews back to school accompanied by a note explaining that she returns all their clothes except *eleven* shirts, not yet washed.

If the clothes of boys were troublesome, those of girls were more so. Madam Mason, as guardian of her children, sends in an account, wherein the support of each child is reckoned at a thousand pounds of tobacco yearly. Her son, Thomson, is charged with linen and ruffled shirts, and her daughter, Mary, with wooden-heeled shoes, petticoats, one hoop-petticoat, and linen. We may be sure that the needling on those petticoats and ruffled skirts would be a reproach, in its dainty fineness, to the machine-made garments of our age.

Little Dolly Payne, who afterward became Mrs. Madison and mistress of the White House, trotted off to school in her childhood (so her biographer tells us), equipped with "a white linen mask to keep every ray of sunshine from the complexion, a sun-bonnet sewed on her head every morning by her careful mother, and long gloves covering the hands and arms."

Gentlewomen, big and little, in ye olden time, seem to have had an inordinate fear of the sunshine, as is evidenced by their long gloves, their veils, and those riding-masks of cloth or velvet, which must have been most uncomfortable to keep in place, even with the aid of the little silver mouth-pieces held between the teeth. But vanity enables people to endure many ills. In a correspondence between Miss Anna Bland in Virginia, and her brother Theodorick in London, the young lady writes: "My Papa has sent for me a dress and a pair of stays. I should be glad if you will be peticular (*sic*) in the choice of them. Let the stays be very stiff bone, and much gored at the hips, and the dress any other color except yellow."

No doubt, the consciousness of looking well, sustained the young martyr, as she gasped through the minuet, in her new dress and her stiff stays, drawn tight at home by the aid of the bed-post. The first directions to the attendant in a case of swooning, so common in our great-grandmothers' lifetime, was to cut the stays, that the imprisoned lungs might get room to breathe once more.

Human nature is oddly inconsistent. These people, who found it incomprehensible that savages should tattoo their bodies, hang beads round their necks, and wear ornaments of snakes and rats hung by the tails through their ears and noses, decked themselves with jewelry, wore wigs and patches, and pierced their ears for barbaric rings of gold or precious stones. I protest I don't know which would have looked queerer to the other, the Indian squaw or the Colonial belle of the eighteenth century; but, from the artistic standpoint, the advantage was all with the child of nature.

In a grave business letter, written to Washington on matters of state by George Mason, the correspondent adds: "P.S. I shall take it as a particular favor if you'll be kind enough to get me two pairs of gold snaps made at Williamsburg, for my little girls. They are small rings with a joint in them, to wear in the ears, instead of ear-rings— also a pair of toupée tongs."

It is a pleasant glimpse we thus gain of one great statesman writing to another, and turning away from public enterprises to remember the private longings of the two little maidens at home, whose hearts are to be gladdened, though the flesh suffers, by these bits of finery.

It was not little girls alone who were willing to endure discomfort in the cause of personal appearance. Washington's false teeth still remain, a monument of his fortitude. They are a set of "uppers and unders" carved in ivory, inserted in a ponderous plate, with clamps in the roof that must have caused torture to the inexperienced mouth. The upper set is connected with the lower by a spiral spring, and the two are arranged to be held in place by the tongue. No one but the hero of Trenton and Valley Forge, could have borne such an affliction and preserved his equanimity.

Tooth-brushes are a modern luxury. In the old times, the most genteel were content to rub the teeth with a rag covered with chalk or snuff, and there was more than a suspicion of effeminacy in a man's cleaning his teeth at all. It is not strange that there was such a demand for the implanted teeth which Dr. Le Mayeur introduced toward the end of the century.

I think it may be fairly claimed that the nineteenth century has marked a great advance in personal cleanliness. To this, as much as anything, except perhaps the use of rubber clothing, we owe its increase of longevity. It is impossible to overestimate the importance to modern hygiene of water-proof substances, keeping the feet and body dry. Pattens and clogs were of service in their day and generation, but they were a clumsy contrivance as compared with the light overshoes of India-rubber. It was not till 1772 that the first efforts were made in Baltimore to introduce the use of umbrellas. "These, like tooth-brushes," writes Scharf, "were at first ridiculed as effeminate, and were only introduced by the vigorous efforts of the doctors, who recommended them chiefly as shields from the sun and a defence against vertigo and prostration from heat. The first umbrellas came from India. They were made of coarse oiled linen, stretched over sticks of rattan, and were heavy and clumsy, but they marked a wonderful step in the direction of hygienic dress. Before their introduction, ministers and doctors, who, more than any one else in the community, were called to face the winter rains, wore a cape of oiled linen, called a *roquelaire*."

THE COLONIAL CAVALIER.

If the dress of the period before the Revolution was not hygienic, it was handsome, and eminently picturesque, as the old portraits of the last century show. The universally becoming ruffles of lace were in vogue, and women still young wore dainty caps, whose delicate lace, falling over the hair, lent softness and youth to the features. Old ladies were not unknown as now, but, at an age when the nineteenth century woman of fashion is still frisking about in the costume of a girl of twenty, the Colonial dame adopted the dress and manners which she conceived suited to her age and dignity. Here, for instance, is the evidence of a portrait, marked on the stretcher, "Amy Newton, aged 45, 1770, John Durand, *pinxit.*" The lady wears an ermine-trimmed cloak draped about her shoulders, over a bodice, lace-trimmed and cut square in the neck. The lace-bordered cap falls as usual over the matron's hair. There is, to me, something rather fine and dignified in the assumption of a matronly dress as a matter of pride and choice. In one respect the Colonial dames, old and young, were gayly attired. Their feet were clad in rainbow hues of brilliant reds and greens and their dresses were generally cut to show to advantage the high-heeled slipper and clocked stocking of bright color.

Washington's order-book forms an excellent guide to the prevailing modes of the day. The orders call for rich coats and waistcoats and cocked hats for himself; and for Mrs. Washington, a salmon tabby velvet, fine flowered lawn aprons, white callimancos hoes, perfumed powder, puckered petticoats, and black velvet riding masks. Master Custis is fitted out with two hair bags and a whole piece of ribbon, while the servants are provided with fifty ells of *osnabergs* (a coarse cloth made of flax and tow manufactured at Osnaberg, in Germany, and much in vogue for servants' wear).

The goods of the time, for high and low, were made to outlast more than one generation. Charles Carroll, of Carrollton, was betrothed in his youth to a beautiful young lady. The wedding-dress was ordered from London, but before its arrival the bride elect had died, and the dress was laid aside. A century later, it appeared at a fancy dress ball, its fabric untarnished, and untouched by time. It was worth while to pay high prices for such stuffs. In many a household to-day is cherished some bit of the brocades, sarcenets, shalloons, and tammies worn by our great-grandmothers and their mothers.

In the Maryland *Gazette*, somewhere in the middle of the last century, Catherine Rathel, milliner, from London, advertises a tempting assortment of white satin, India and other chintzes, calico, gingham, cloaks, cardinal's hats, flowered gauze aprons, bonnets, caps, égrettes, fillets, breast-flowers, fashionable ribbands, buttons and loops, silk hose, superfine white India stockings, box and ivory combs.

The firm of Rivington & Brown present an equally attractive display for gentlemen: "An importation of hats, gold and silver-laced, and *cocked by his Majesty's Hatter*. London-made pumps and boot-garters, silk or buff sword-belts and gorgets, newest style paste shoe-buckles, gold seals, snuff-boxes of tortoise-shell, leather, or papier-maché."

Whatever luxuries or elegances of the toilet a man of fashion might possess, his snuff-box was his chief pride. This was the weapon with which he fought the bloodless battles of the drawing-room and, armed with it, he felt himself a Cavalier indeed. The nice study of the times and seasons when it should be tapped, when played with, when offered or accepted, and when haughtily thrust into the pocket, marked the gentleman of the old school. But one use of the snuff-box, I am certain, was never devised by either Steele or Lilie, but was left for the brain or nerves of a Colonial dame to invent. A widow, left alone and unprotected, occupied that ground-floor room generally designated in the Colonial house as the parlor-chamber. Fearing firearms more than robbers, she armed herself with a large snuff-box, which, in case of any suspicious noise in the night, she was wont to click loudly, in imitation of the cocking of a gun. The effect on the hypothetical robbers was instantaneous, and they never disturbed her twice in the same night.

Colonial dress, as we advance toward the time of the Revolution, grows simpler. Wigs fall by their own weight, and men begin to wear their own hair, drawn back and fastened in dignified fashion with a bow of broad ribbon, generally black. Except for ruffled shirts and deep cuffs, the costume of society approaches the sobriety of to-day, and the lack of money and threat of war subdue the dress even of the women. The military alone still keep up the pomp and circumstance of costume worn by all men in the Stuart era. In 1774, the Fairfax Independent Company of Volunteers meet in Virginia, and resolve to gather at stated seasons for practice of military exercise and discipline. It is further resolved that their dress shall be a uniform of blue turned up with buff, with plain yellow metal buttons, buff waistcoat, and breeches, and white stockings; and furnished with good flint-lock and bayonet, sling cartouch box and tomahawk.

Washington's orders from Fort Cumberland, dated the seventeenth of September, 1775, prescribe the uniform to be worn by the Virginia

Regiment in the opening struggle: "Every officer of the Virginia Regiment to provide himself, as soon as he can conveniently, with suit of Regimentals of good blue Cloath; the Coat to be faced and cuffed with scarlet, and trimmed with Silver; a scarlet waistcoat, with silver Lace; blue Breeches, and a silver-laced hat, if to be had, for Camp or Garrison duty. Besides this, each officer to provide himself with a common soldier's Dress for Detachments and Duty in the Woods."

In looking back to the beginning of the Revolutionary War, when that great wrench was made which separated America from the parent country, we have a feeling that men's minds were wholly occupied with the tremendous issues at stake; yet, as we study the old records, we find the same buying and selling, the planting and reaping, the same pondering and planning of dress and the trifles of daily life going on much in the old fashion. In Jefferson's private note-book, under date of July 4th, 1776, the day of the signing of the Declaration of Independence, I find, entered in his own hand, the item: "For seven pairs of women's gloves, twenty shillings."

Even so do great things and small jostle one another in this strange world of ours, and a woman's glove lies close to the document which changed the fate of nations.

News, Trade and Travel

News, Trade, and Travell

IN the early days, the highways of the Cavalier Colonies were the broad waters of bay and sound; their by-ways, the innumerable rivers and creeks; and their toll-gates, the ports of entry. Road-making was tedious and costly, and the settlers saw no reason for wasting time and energy in the undertaking, when nature had spread her pathways at their feet, and they needed only to step into a canoe, or a skiff manned by black oarsmen, to glide from one plantation to another; or to hoist sail in a pinnace for distant settlements. Many animals travel, but man is the only one who packs a trunk, and, except a few like the nautilus and the squirrel, the only one who sails a boat. There is a sentiment connected with a ship, which no other conveyance can ever have. The very names of those old colonial vessels are redolent of "amber-greece," "pearle," and treasure, of East India spices and seaweed

> "From Bermuda's reefs, and edges
> Of sunken ledges
> In some far-off bright Azore."

THE COLONIAL CAVALIER.

The history of the colonies might be written in the story of their ships. There were *The Good Speed*, *The Discovery*, and *The Susan Constant*, which preceded the world-famous *Half Moon* and *Mayflower* to the new world. There were *The Ark* and *The Dove* that brought over Lord Baltimore and his colonists; *The Sea-Venture* which went to wreck on the Somer Isles; and *The Patience*, and *The Deliverance* which brought her crew safe to Virginia. These were the pioneers, followed by a long line of staunch craft, large and small, from the *Golden Lyon* to *The Peggy Stewart*, which discharged her cargo of taxed tea into Chesapeake Bay.

Many ships in those days were named, as we name chrysanthemums, in honor of some prominent man or fair dame. These good folk must have followed the coming and going of their namesakes with curious interest. The sight of a sail on the horizon never lost its excitement, for every ship brought some wild tale of adventure. The story of shipwreck "on the still vexed Bermoothes," and the wonderful escape of Gates and Somers, with their crew, has been made famous forever by the tradition that it suggested to Shakespeare the plot of *The Tempest;* but every "frygat" that touched at Jamestown or Annapolis brought accounts almost as thrilling, of storm and stress, of fighting tempests with a crew reduced by scurvy to three or four active seamen, of running for days from a Spanish caravel or a French pickaroune.

The *Margaret and John* set sail for America early in the seventeenth century, carrying eighty passengers, besides sailors, and armed with "eight Iron peeces and a Falcon." When she reached the "Ile of Domenica," the captain entered a harbor, that the men might stretch their limbs on dry land, "having been eleven weeks pestered in this vnwholesome ship." Here, to their misfortune, they found two large ships flying Hollander colors, but proving to be Spaniards. These enemies sent a volley of shot which split the oars and made holes in the boats, yet failed to strike a man on the *Margaret and John*.

"Perceiving what they were," writes one of the English crew, "we fitted ourselves the best we could to prevent a mischief: seeing them warp themselves to windward, we thought it not good to be boarded on both sides at an anchor; we intended to set saile, but the Vice-Admiral battered so hard at our starboard side, that we fell to our businesse, and answered their vnkindnesse with such faire shot from a demiculvering, that shot her betweene wind and water, whereby she was glad to leave us and her Admirall together." The Admiral then bespoke them, and demanded a surrender; to which the sturdy English replied that they had no quarrel with the King of Spain, and asked only to go their way unmolested, but as they would do no wrong, assuredly they would take none. The Spaniards answered these bold words with another volley of shot, returned with energy by the English guns.

"The fight continued halfe an houre, as if we had been invironed with fire and smoke, untill they discovered the waste of our ship naked, where they bravely boorded us, loofe for loofe, hasting with pikes and swords to enter; but it pleased God so to direct our Captaine and encourage our men with valour, that our pikes being formerly placed under our halfe deck, and certaine shot lying close for that purpose under the port holes, encountered them so rudely, that their fury was not onely rebated, but their hastinesse intercepted, and their whole company beaten backe; many of our men were hurt, but I am sure they had two for one." Thus, all day and all night, the unequal battle continued, till at length the doughty little British vessel fairly fought off her two enemies, and they fell sullenly back and ran near shore to mend their leaks, while the *Margaret and John* stood on her course.

It is hard, in these days, when the high seas are as safe as city streets, to realize the condition of terror to which merchantmen were reduced, two hundred years ago, by the rumor of a black flag seen in the offing, or of some "pyrat" lying in wait outside the harbor. In Governor Spotswood's time, Williamsburg was thrown into a state of great excitement by the report that the dreaded buccaneer John Theach, known by the name of Blackbeard, had been seen cruising along the coasts of Virginia and Carolina. The Governor rose to the occasion, however. He sent out Lieutenant Maynard with two ships, to look for Blackbeard. Maynard found him and boarded his vessel in Pamlico Sound. The pirate was no coward. He ordered one of his men to stand beside the powder-magazine with a lighted match, ready, at a signal from him, to blow up friends and foes together. The signal never came, for a lucky shot killed Blackbeard on the spot and his crew surrendered. They might as well have died with their leader, for thirteen of them were hanged at Williamsburg. Blackbeard's skull was rimmed with silver and made into a ghastly drinking-cup, and we hear no more of pirates in those waters.

The protection of vessels was not the only reason for policing the waterways. Smuggling was much more common than piracy, and the laws against it were the harder to enforce, because the entire community was secretly in sympathy with

THE COLONIAL CAVALIER.

the offenders. In the earliest Maryland records is Lord Baltimore's commission, giving his lieutenant authority to "appoint fit places for public ports for lading, shipping, unlading and discharging all goods and merchandizes to be imported or exported into or out of our said province, and to prohibit the shipping or discharging of any goods or merchandizes whatsoever in all other places." Any one violating the shipping law was subject to heavy fines and imprisonment.

In Virginia the statutes compelled ships to stop at Jamestown, or other designated ports, before breaking bulk at the private landings along the river. Who can picture the excitement in those lonely plantations when the frigate tied up at the wharf, and began to unload from its hold, its cargo of tools for the farm, furniture for the house, and, best of all, the square white letters with big round seals, containing news of the friends distant a three months' journey! Sometimes the new comer would prove no ocean voyager, but a nearer neighbor, some stout, round-sterned packet, from New Netherland or New England, laden with grain and rum, or hides and rum, to be exchanged for the tobacco of the Old Dominion.

To journey from one colony to another thus, the trader must first secure a license and take oath that he would not sell or give arms or ammunition to the Indians. On these terms Lord Baltimore, in 1637, granted to a merchant mariner, liberty "to trade and commerce for corn, beaver or any other commodities with the Dutchmen on Hudson's river, or with any Indians or other people whatsoever being or inhabiting to the northward, without the capes commonly called Cape Henry and Cape Charles."

Long after the waters of Chesapeake Bay were dotted with sails, and the creeks of Maryland and Virginia gay with skiffs, the land communication was still in an exceedingly primitive condition. The roads were little more than bridle-paths. The surveyors deemed their duty done if the logs and fallen trees were cleared away, and all Virginia could not boast of a single engineer. Bridges there were none; and the traveller, arriving at a river bank, must find a ford, or swim his horse across, counting himself fortunate if he kept his pouch of tobacco dry. Planters at a distance from the rivers hewed out rolling-roads, on which they brought down their tobacco in casks, attached to the horses that drew them by hoop-pole shafts. Roads, winding along the streams, were slowly laid out, and answered well enough in fair weather, but in storms they were impassable, and at night so bewildering that belated travellers were forced to come to a halt, make a fire, and bivouac till morning. In 1704, the roads in Maryland were so poor that we find the Assembly passing an act declaring that "the roads leading to any county court-house shall have two notches on the trees on both sides of the roads, and another notch a distance above the other two; and any road that leads to any church shall be marked, into the entrance of the same, and at the leaving any other road, with a slip cut down the face of the tree near the ground." Guide-posts were still unknown.

The travel was as primitive as the roads. Public coaches did not exist. Horseback riding was the usual way of getting over the ground, though the rough roads made the jolting a torment. "Travelling in this country," wrote a stranger, as late as the Revolution, "is extremely dangerous, especially if it is the least windy, from the number of rotten pines continually blowing down." It was no uncommon thing for a driver to be obliged to turn into the woods half a dozen times in a single mile to avoid the fallen logs. A certain Madame de Reidefel, who was driving in a post-chaise with her children, had a narrow escape from death. A rotten tree fell directly across her path, but fortunately struck between the chaise and the horses, so that the occupants of the carriage escaped, though the

front wheels were crushed, and one of the horses lamed.

Between pirates on sea and pine-trees on land, so many perils beset the traveller that starting on a journey became a momentous undertaking. "It was no uncommon thing," writes the historian, "for one who went on business or pleasure from Charleston to Boston or New York, if he were a prudent and cautious man, to consult the almanac before setting out, to make his will, to give a dinner or a supper to his friends at the tavern, and there to bid them a formal goodbye."

A journey being so great an affair, the traveller was of course a marked man, and his arrival at an ordinary was the signal for the gathering of all who could crowd in to hear of his adventures, and also to hear the public and private news of which he might be the bearer. "I have heard Dr. Franklin relate with great pleasantry," said one of his friends, "that in travelling when he was young, the first step he took for his tranquillity and to obtain immediate attention at the inns, was to anticipate inquiry, by saying: 'My name is Benjamin Franklin. I was born at Boston, am a printer by profession, am travelling to Philadelphia, shall have to return at such a time, and have no news. Now what can you give me for dinner?'"

This curiosity was rather peculiar to New England. The Southerner, while perhaps as anxious to hear the news, was more restrained in asking questions. That good breeding and tact which were a Cavalier inheritance, taught him to wait decorously for his news as for his food. A foreigner in the last century, in travelling through the South, came upon a party of Virginians smoking and drinking together on a veranda. He reports that on his ascending the steps to the piazza, every countenance seemed to say, 'This man has a double claim to our attention, for he is a stranger in the place!' In a moment, there was room made for him to sit down; a new bowl was called for, and every one who addressed him did it with a smile of conciliation; but no man asked him whence he had come or whither he was going."

All foreigners bear the same testimony to this universal courtesy, which smoothed rough roads and made travelling enjoyable, in spite of its difficulties and dangers. When I realize what those difficulties were, I am surprised at the willingness with which journeys were undertaken. I read of Washington setting out on a mission to Major-General Shirley in Boston, and riding the whole distance of five hundred miles on horseback in the depth of winter, escorted only by a few servants; yet little is made of his experiences. Women, too, were quite accustomed to riding on long expeditions. An octogenarian described to Irving the horseback journeys of his mother in her scarlet cloth riding-habit. "Young ladies from the country," he said, "used to come to the balls at Annapolis, riding, with their hoops arranged *fore and aft* like lateen sails; and after dancing all night, would ride home again in the morning."

Annapolis, before the Revolution, was a centre of gayety. Its rich families came up to town for the season each Fall, and in the Spring moved back to their country-houses with their various belongings. The family coach which was used to transport these possessions was a curious affair to modern eyes. It was colored generally a light yellow, with smart facings. The body was of mahogany, with Venetian windows on each side, projecting lamps, and a high seat upon which coachman and footman climbed at starting.

As this old coach lumbered up and down the streets of Annapolis, its occupants no doubt fancied that they had reached the final limit of speed and comfort in travel, and they looked back with scorn and pity on the primitive conveyances of their ancestors, just as posterity will doubtless look back from their balloons and electric motors on our steam engines. In one of Jefferson's early letters we chance upon a curious prophecy. Being about to make a visit, he asks to be met by his friend's "periagua," as a canoe was called, and suggests that some day a boat may be made, which shall row itself.

After all, I question whether there was not more pleasure in travel in those days, before boats rowed themselves, and when horses were made of flesh and blood instead of iron and steam; when the rider ambled along, noting each tree and shrub, pausing to exchange greetings with every wayfarer, and stopping by night beneath some hospitable roof to make merry over the cup of sack or the glass of "quince drink" prepared for his refreshment. If the traveller was of a surly and unsocial nature, he was indeed to be pitied; since, for him who would not accept his neighbor's hospitality, there remained only the roadside tavern or "ordinary," and woe to him who was compelled to test its welcome! The universal practice of keeping open-house made the inns poorer in quality, and the contempt of the community for one who would receive money for the entertainment of guests, kept men of repute out of the business.

A Maryland statute, in 1674, resolves "that noe Person in that Province shall have a Licence to keep Ordinary for the future but th^t he shall give Bond to his Excellency with good Sureties that he shall keep foure good ffeather beds for the Entertainment of Customers." In any place where the county court is held, he is directed to keep "eight ffeather or fflock beds at the least, and ffurniture suitable." The charges of the ordinary-keeper are fixed by law. He is allowed to charge ten pounds of tobacco per meal "for dyet," ten pounds "for small beare," and four "for lodging *in a bed with sheets.*"

While the traveller was loitering on the road, enjoying hospitality or enduring ordinaries, those he left at home were in ignorance of his whereabouts; and it was only after days or weeks of anxious waiting, that they could hope to hear of his safe arrival at his destination. Meanwhile rumor, which always thrives in proportion to ignorance, might make their lives miserable by reports of a riderless horse seen galloping into some village, of storms and gales, or of trees crashing across the lonely roads. In the absence of the post and the telegraph, this spreading of false news became so troublesome that an act was passed in Maryland declaring that, " Whereas many Idle and Bussie-headed people doe forge and divulge falce Rumors and Reports," it is enacted that they be either fined or "receive such corporall punishment, not extending to life or member, as to the Iustices of that court shall seeme meete."

THE COLONIAL CAVALIER.

It was long before the idea of a postal service under government control dawned upon the Colonies. Throughout almost the whole of the seventeenth century letters were sent by the hand of the chance traveller. Maryland directed that in the case of public state-papers the sheriff of one county should carry them to the sheriff of the next, and so on to their goal; but private letters had no such official care.

An old Virginia statute commanded that "all letters superscribed *for the publique service*, should be immediately conveyed from plantation to plantation to the place and person directed, under the penalty of one hogshead of tobacco for each default."

Another law, bearing date 1661, orders that "when there is any person in the family where the letters come, as can write, such person is required to endorse the day and houre he received them, that the neglect or contempt of any person stopping them may be the better knowne and punished accordingly."

A letter in those days merited the attention it received, for it represented a vast deal of labor and expense. Paper was a costly luxury, as we may infer from those old yellow pages crossed and re-crossed with writing, and the tiny cramped hand in which the old sermons are written. In 1680, I find Colonel William Fitzhugh ordering from London "two large Paper-Books, one to contain about fourteen or fifteen quires of paper, the other about ten quires, and one other small one."

The paper was left blank on one side, and so folded that it formed its own envelope. It was fastened with a seal whose taste and elegance was a matter of pride with the writer. The style was formal, as became the dignity of a person who knew how to write. In those times people did not write letters; they indited epistles. A communication sent across the ocean, in 1614, is addressed "To ye Truly Honorable & Right Worthy Knight, Sr Thomas Smith," and is signed: "At Y^r Command To Be Disposed of."

Love-letters shared the formality of the time, and were written with a stateliness and elaboration of compliment which suggest a minuet on paper. Family letters are often in the form of a journal, and cover a period of months. They cost both labor and money but they were worth their price. Cheap postage has made cheap writing. We no longer compose; we only scribble.

In 1693, Thomas Neale was appointed by royal patent, "postmaster-general of Virginia and *all other parts of North America.*" The House of Burgesses passed an Act declaring that if post-offices were established in every county, Neale should receive threepence for every letter not exceeding one sheet, or to or from any place not exceeding four score English miles distance.

In 1706, letters were forwarded eight times a year from Philadelphia to the Potomac, and afterward as far as Williamsburg, with the proviso that the post-rider should not start for Philadelphia till he had received enough letters to pay the expenses of the trip.

The average day's journey for a postman covered a distance of some forty miles in Summer, and over good roads; but, when the heavy Autumn rains washed out great gullies in his path or the Winter storms beat him back, he was lucky if he accomplished half that distance. His letters were subject to so many accidents, that it is a wonder they ever reached the persons to whom they were addressed. It was not till the post-office passed into Franklin's energetic and methodical hands that it was made regular and trustworthy.

The estimate of the common post in early days

is curiously illustrated by an episode which occurred in Virginia. The hero was one Mr. Daniel Park, "who," says the chronicle, "to all the other accomplishments that make a complete sparkish gentleman, has added one upon which he infinitely values himself; that is, a quick resentment of every, the least thing, that looks like an affront or injury."

One September morning, when the Governor of Maryland was breakfasting with Mr. Commissary Blair at Middle Plantation, Colonel Park marched in upon them, having a sword about him, much longer than what he commonly travelled with, and which he had caused to be ground sharp in the point that morning. Addressing himself to the Governor of Maryland, he burst out: "Captain Nicholson, did you receive a letter that I sent you from New York?"

"Yes," answered Nicholson, "I received it."

"And was it done like a gentleman," fumed the fiery colonel, "to send that letter by the hand of a common post, to be read by everybody in Virginia? I look upon it as an affront, and expect satisfaction!"

Fancy the number of affairs of honor that this "complete young sparkish gentleman" would have on hand if he lived in the present year of grace and resented every letter sent him by *the common post!*

THE COLONIAL CAVALIER.

There is something which strikes us as infinitely diverting in his suggestion that everybody in Virginia would be interested in his letter. But perhaps he was nearer the truth than we realize, for in his day all news came through such sources, and a letter was regarded as a good thing, which it would be gross selfishness not to share with one's neighbors. As for a letter from Europe it was an affair of the greatest magnitude, exciting the interest of the whole community.

Those giant folios which entertain us every morning with their gossip from all quarters of the globe had no existence then. Early in the last century, the Colonial Cavalier gleaned all his knowledge of the world and its affairs, from some three-month-old copy of the London papers and magazines, brought over by a British packet. Even this communication, it seems, was uncertain, for complaint is made that the masters of vessels keep the packages till an accidental conveyance offers, and for want of better opportunities frequently commit them to boatmen, who care very little for their goods, so they get their freight.

The colonists had struggled to establish a local journal, and a printing press had been started in Virginia in the seventeenth century, but it had been strangled in its infancy by Berkeley, who declared it the parent of treason and infidelity; and so it came about that the Southern Provinces had no public utterance for their news or their views, till the silence was broken by the voice of Maryland, speaking through her *Gazette*, in 1727, when in all America there were only six rival sheets. Franklin says that his brother's friends tried to dissuade him from publishing *The New England Courant*, on the ground that there was already one newspaper in America. His memory lapsed a little, as *The Courant* had in fact three predecessors, but the incident shows how little notion there was at that time, of the public demand for news.

In 1736, was first issued *The Virginia Gazette*, a dingy little sheet about twelve by six inches in size, and costing to subscribers, fifteen shillings a year. The newspaper of the day had no editorial page. Its comments on public affairs were in the form of letters, after the fashion of *The Tatler* and *The Spectator*. It had a poet's corner, where many a young versemaker tried the wings of his Pegasus, and it printed also poetical tributes under the notices of deaths and marriages. In this section, after the record of the wedding of Mr. William Derricoat and Miss Suckie Tomkies, appear these lines:

> "Hers the mild lustre of the blooming morn
> And his the radiance of the rising day—
> Long may they live and mutually possess
> A steady love and genuine happiness!"

When Edmund Randolph married Betsey Nicholas, the poet found himself unable to express his emotions in less than two stanzas:

"Exalted theme, too high for common lays!
Could my weak muse with beauty be inspired,
In numbers smooth I'd chant my Betsy's praise,
And tell how much her Randolph is admired.

"To light the hymeneal torch, since they're resolved,
Kind Heaven, I trust, will make them truly blest;
And when the Gordian knot shall be dissolved,
Translate them to eternal peace and rest."

It is safe to say that this figure, comparing matrimony with a Gordian knot, was original with the poet. Had the bridegroom been as fiery and "sparkish" as Colonel Park, he might have called out the writer, but he seems to have taken it in good part.

The prospectus of the Maryland *Gazette* for 1745 announces that its price will be twelve shillings a year, or fourteen shillings sealed and delivered. It promises the freshest advices, foreign and domestic, but adds, with much simplicity and candor: "In a dearth of news, which in this remote part of the world may sometimes reasonably be expected, we shall study to supply the deficit by presenting our readers with the best material we can possibly collect, having always due regard to the promotion of virtue and learning, the suppression of vice and immorality, and the instruction as well as entertainment of our readers." What more could the most exacting subscriber demand?

Advertisements, then, as now, served the double purpose of filling space, and supporting the paper. They were charged for, at the rate of five shillings for the first week, and one shilling for each week following, provided they were of moderate length—a vague provision, one would say. These old advertisements are of great value to the student of the life of the past. They give a better picture of the condition of society, than a ream of "notes." Here we read of the shipping of a crew on a packet bound for England. Half-way down the column a lost hog is advertised, and here, Edward Morris, breeches-maker, announces a sale of buckskin breeches, and gloves with high tops, and assures his customers that "they may depend on kind usage at reasonable rates." Surely the resources of modern advertising have never devised anything more alluring than this promise of "kind usage at reasonable rates."

Since the art of reading was unknown to a considerable proportion of the community, it was natural that pictorial devices should be largely used. Not only were the shops along the highways distinguished by such signs as "the Blue Glove," and "the Golden Keys," with appropriate illustrations; but in the advertising columns of the papers, the print was re-enforced by pictures of ships and horses, and runaway slaves.

The purchase and sale of negroes formed a standing advertisement, beneath the caption of an auction-block.

In the Virginia *Gazette* of August, 1767, we find the following under the curious headline:

"SALE OF A MUSICAL SLAVE."

"A valuable young handsome Negro fellow, about 18 or 20 years of age; has every qualification of a genteel and sensible servant, and has been in many different parts of the world. He shaves, dresses hair, and plays on the French horn. He lately came from London, and has with him two suits of new clothes, which the purchaser may have with him. Inquire at the printing office."

It is hard to understand why the owner should wish to part with a prodigy possessed of so many accomplishments. Perhaps his playing on the French horn is the explanation.

Runaway servants, both black and white, form the subject of many advertisements in those old newspapers. In the Maryland *Gazette* (1769) appears a description in rhyme of the disappearance of an indented servant:

> "Last Wednesday morn at break of day,
> From Philadelphia ran away
> An Irishman, named John McKeogn.
> To fraud and imposition prone,
> About five feet five inches high;
> Can curse and swear, as well as lie.
> How old he is I can't engage,
> But forty-five is near his age.
>
> "He oft in conversation chatters
> Of Scripture and religious matters,
> And fain would to the world impart
> That virtue lodges in his heart.
> But, take the rogue from stem to stern,
> The hypocrite you'll soon discern
>
> "And find, though his deportment's civil,
> A saint without, within a devil.
> Whoe'er secures said John McKeogn,
> (Provided I should get my own),
> Shall have from me in cash paid down
> Five dollar bills, and half-a-crown."

Mary Nelson is the owner and poet, or, in the fashion of the day, I should say poetess, and perhaps *owneress*, as I find it recorded of Mary Goddard that she was postmistress of Baltimore and *Printress* and *Editress* of the *Baltimore Journal*.

The world moves. The auction-block, and the

runaway slave, with his bundle on his back, have disappeared from among the pictures in the advertising column; the packet has given way to the ocean steamer; the horse to the bicycle; the stage coach to the railroad; the little provincial gazettes, with their coarse gray paper and blurred type, to the great dailies, as large as the Bible and as doubtful as the Apocrypha. I wonder if another century will have such astounding tales to tell of progress in news, trade and travel!

His Friends and Foes

His Friendes and Foes.

THE early adventurers had never seen anything of savage life till they touched the shores of Virginia. Everything connected with the strange beings there was full of interest. They set down faithfully whatever they saw, and a good deal more besides.

The Susquehannocks impressed them most of all the Indian tribes. Their enormous height and fine proportions made them look like giants, and their attire was as impressive as their persons. One who saw them, writes home in those first pioneer days: "Their attire is the skinnes of Beares and Woolves. Some have Cassacks made of Beares heads and skinnes that a mans head goes through the skinnes neck, and the eares of the Beare fastened to his shoulders, the nose and teeth hanging downe his breast, another Beares face split behind him, and at the end of the nose hung a Pawe. The half sleeves comming to the elbowes were the neckes of Beares and the armes through the mouth with pawes hanging at their noses. One had the head of a Wolfe hanging in a chaine for a Iewell."

One of their chiefs specially impressed the English. He was a giant among giants. The calf of his leg was three-quarters of a yard round, and "the rest of his limbs answerable to that proportion." His arrows were five quarters long, and he wore a wolf's skin at his back for a quiver. The picture of this Indian Hercules accompanied the maps which Captain Smith sent home to enlighten the Company in England.

The stories of the different adventurers were gathered together and printed as "The General History of Virginia." The volume was adorned (I cannot say illustrated) by a series of woodcuts, which make us laugh aloud by their inaccuracy. The Indians are simply gigantic Englishmen naked and beardless, with the hair standing in a stiff ridge on top of the head, like a cock's comb. The wigwams look like haystacks, and the canoes like bathtubs. What a collection of pictures we might have had, if a kodak had been among the possessions of Captain Smith and his company! We should see King Pamaunche with "the chaine of pearles round his necke thrice double, the third parte of them as bygg as pease," and catch a view of his "pallace" with its hundred-acre garden set with beans, pease, tobacco, gourdes, pompions, "and other thinges unknowne to us in our tongue." We should have the interiors of the smoky wigwams which Spelman and Archer visited, the forms of the squaws dimly outlined against the grimy mat, as they pounded corn, or dropped the bread into the kettle to boil.

Thanks to John Smith's graphic pen, we have a picture of Powhatan, that fierce old ancestor of so many first families of Virginia, almost as vivid as a photograph. Smith went to visit him, and found him proudly lying upon a bedstead a foot high, upon ten or twelve mats. "At head sat a woman, at his feet another. On each side, sitting upon a mat upon the ground, were ranged his chief men, on each side the fire, five or ten in rank, and behind them as many young women, each a great chaine of white beads over their shoulders, their heads painted in red, and with such a grave and majestical countenance as drove us into admiration to see such state in a naked savage."

We might suppose these last words applied to the women, instead of to Powhatan, did we not know how little state and majesty were allowed these copper-colored Griseldas. The Indian squaws were little more than slaves. When the braves moved, it was the squaws who carried the wigwams and set them up in the new camp. When the men sat at meals, they spread the mats, waited upon their masters, and finally contented their appetites with the remnants of the feast. In the field, too, they bore the brunt of the toil: "Let squaws and hedgehogs scratch the ground," said an old warrior; "man was made for war and the chase."

Yet, wretched and abused as these women were, they seemed content with their lot, and when their husbands died, they not only mourned for them, but seemed quite ready to enter the same servitude with a new master. "I once saw a young widow," said Jefferson, "whose husband, a warrior, had died about eight days before, hastening to finish her grief, and who, by tearing her hair, beating her breast, and drinking spirits, made the tears flow in great abundance in order that she might grieve much in a short space of time, and be married that evening to another young warrior."

Spelman, a Virginia adventurer who, in the course of one of his exploring trips, witnessed an Indian wedding, has left us an account of the ceremony. "Ye man," he says, "goes not unto any place to be married, but ye woman is brought to him where he dwelleth. At her coming, her father or cheefe frend ioynes the hands togither, and then ye father, or cheefe frend of the man, bringeth a longe string of beades and, measuringe his armes leangth thereof, doth breake it over ye handes of those that ar to be married while their handes be ioyned together and gives it unto ye woman's father or him that brings hir. And so, with much mirth and feastinge they go togither."

This "longe string of beades" of which Spelman spoke, was probably made of the *peak* and *roanoke*, which made the riches of the Indian, and served him at once for money and ornament. Both were made from shell—one dark, the other white. The darker was the more valuable, and was distinguished as *wampum* peak. The English traders accepted it as coinage, and reckoned its value at eighteen pence a yard, while the white peak sold for ninepence. In the proceedings of the Maryland Council we find Thomas Cornwaleys licensed to trade with the Indians for corn, roanoke, and peak.

When the red men wished to make bargains with the English, before interpreters had been trained to speak both languages, the counting was done by dropping beans, one by one, amid total silence. Woe to the offender who interrupted an Indian during this critical operation, or indeed at any time! An interruption was looked upon as an unpardonable affront. Once, in the time of Bacon's Rebellion, an Indian chief, accompanied by several of his tribe, came to negotiate a treaty of peace with the English. In the course of the Werrowance's address, one of his attendants ventured to put in a word. Instantly, the chief snatched a tomahawk from his girdle, split the poor fellow's skull, motioned to his companions to carry him out, and continued his speech as calmly as though nothing had happened.

The lack of ceremony in the white men's address, and the frequency with which they interrupted, struck the Indian as amazing and unpardonable. There is a tradition that one of the early preachers strove to teach an old Indian brave the doctrine of the Trinity. The Indian heard him calmly to the end, and then began in his turn to tell of the Great Spirit who spoke in the thunder, and whose smile was the sunshine. In the midst of his discourse, the clergyman broke in, "But all this is not true." The Indian, turning to the circle around, remarked: "What sort of man is this? He has been talking for an hour of his three Gods, and now he will not let me tell of my one."

The character of the Indian was a strange mixture of apparent contradictions. He would hunt and fish for a season, and then feast and make merry night and day while his supplies lasted. When they were exhausted, he would gird up his loins, and fast for a period long enough to end the life of a white man. He had an inordinate love of finery, upon which the English traded from the first. He would barter away a whole Winter's provisions of corn for a scarlet blanket or a bunch of gay-colored beads. Yet he was not without a natural shrewdness which enlightened him when he was being cheated. The story runs that some of the early missionaries taught the savages that their salvation depended on catching for them shad, which they sold to the settlers. In the course of time the Indians discovered the trick, and drove out the deceivers. Years afterward, another mission was established, and the first priest took as his text, "Ho, every one that thirsteth, come ye to the waters!" The Indians gathered round the preacher when the sermon was ended, and one of the tribe said: "White man, you speak in fine words of the waters of life; but before we decide on what we have heard, we would like to know *whether any shad swim in those waters!*"

It must be confessed that the Indians appear to better advantage than the English, in the early transactions. When Hamor went to visit King Powhatan, he was received with royal courtesy. The chief sent one of his attendants to bring what food he could find, though he explained that, as they were not expecting visitors, they had not kept anything ready. "Presently," Hamor recounts, "the bread was brought in two great wodden bowls, the quantity of a bushel sod bread, made up round, of the bygnesse of a tenise-ball, whereof we eat some few." After this repast, Hamor and his comrades were regaled with "a great glasse of sacke," and then were ushered into the wigwam appropriated to them for the night. English and Indian ideas of comfort did not correspond, however, for Hamor complains: " We had not bin halfe an hour in the house, before the fleas began so to torment us that we could not rest there, but went forth and under a broade oake, upon a mat, reposed ourselves that night."

Hamor took with him on this visit, as an offering to the Indian chief, five strings of blue and white beads, two pieces of copper, five wooden combs, ten fishhooks, and a pair of knives. In return for these costly presents, this pious English gentleman asked Powhatan, who had already given Pocahontas to the whites, to send them another daughter, really as a hostage, but nominally as a wife to Sir Thomas Dale, the worthy governor of Virginia, regardless of the slight objection that there was already a Lady Dale in England. Pocahontas had good reason for saying to Smith when she met him in London, " Your countrymen will lie much."

To the early settlers the savage seemed a strange being, not more than half human, who happened to be in possession of the land they coveted. They thought they did God service when they flung to the Indian a Bible and a handful of beads, in exchange for the land which had been his birthright for centuries. They cheated and cajoled him when he was angry, as they might have wheedled an angry tiger; yet, strange to say, they were quite off their guard when, at length, the tiger made his spring, and glutted the vengeance he had been nursing so long.

When the news of the Indian massacre reached England, it roused a frenzy of revenge equal in fury to that of the savages. The Virginia Company quite forgot that they had set forth in their charter that the conversion of the Indians was one of the main objects of the new adventure, or if they remembered it at all, it was only to apologize lamely for a complete change of base. "We condemn their bodies," they wrote to the colonists, "the saving of whose souls we have so zealously affected. Root them out from being any longer a people. . . . War perpetually without peace or truce: yet spare the young for servants" (the Englishman even in a rage has an eye to the main chance). "Starve them by destroying their corn, or reaping it for your own use! Pluck up their weirs! Obstruct their hunting! Employ foreign enemies against them at so much a head! Keep a band of your own men continually upon them, to be paid by the colony, which is to have half of their captives and plunder!"

These short, nervous sentences fell like hammer-strokes on the ears of the Englishmen in America, and they found an echo in their hearts. It is easy for us to characterize their revengeful spirit as inconsistent and unchristian. It is easy to tolerate a bear in a menagerie, or an Indian on a reservation. It is quite another thing to exercise toleration toward either in the life-and-death grip of a frontier struggle.

These men had seen their homes go up in flames. They had heard the blood-curdling war-whoop. They had counted the bloody scalps hanging at the Indian's belt, and marked on them the hair of those they loved. It was idle to preach toleration to them. Henceforward for many years it was war to the knife.

Yet, both as friend and foe, the Indian had given the colonists many lessons. He had taught them the culture of maize and tobacco, he had taught them to stalk the deer, to trap the bear, and to blaze the forest path. Many a lesson in woodcraft the settlers learned from him. Washington's shrewdness in borrowing native methods of warfare, would, had his advice been taken, have saved Braddock's army from utter rout in the Western forests. The very enmity of the Indian was a help to the Colonial Cavalier, whose ease-loving temperament might easily have sunk into sloth had it not felt the spur of danger and the necessity for being on the alert. The docility of the negro was a perpetual temptation to the white man to the abuse of arbitrary power, but the resistance of the Indian was a constant reminder that here was a force unsubdued and unsubduable.

Of the influence of the white men on the Indian, the less said the better. They eradicated none of his vices, and they lent him many of their own. They found him abstinent, and they made him a guzzler of firewater. They found him hospitable, and they made him suspicious and vindictive. They found him in freedom, the owner of a great country; they robbed him of the one, and crowded him out of the other.

An old sachem in the eighteenth century, meeting a surveyor, said to him: "The French claim all the land on one side of the Ohio, the English claim all the land on the other side. Now, where does the Indian's land lie?"

The savages exchanged their corn and tobacco for the rum-cask and the firearms of civilization, and a strange jumble of a new religion, whose ceremonies they grafted onto their own, with grotesque results. It is hard to say whether they fared worst as the white man's friends or foes. When the English made a treaty with the Chickahomanies, "a lustie and a daring people," these were the terms offered them by the whites:

"First: They should for ever bee called Englishmen and bee true subiects to King James and his Deputies.

"Secondly: Neither to kill nor detaine any of our men, nor cattell, but bring them home.

"Thirdly: To bee alwaies ready to furnish us with three hundred men, against the Spaniards or any.

"Fourthly: They shall not enter our townes, but send word they are new Englishmen.

"Fifthly: That every fighting man, at the beginning of harvest shall bring to our store two bushels of corne for tribute, for which they shall receive so many hatchets.

"Lastly: The eight chiefe men should see all this performed or receive the punishment themselves; for their diligence they should have a red coat, a copper chaine, and King James his picture, and be accounted his noblemen."

This shameful bargain is recorded by the English with evident self-satisfaction, and apparently without a suspicion that they need blush for the transaction. Yet when the Indian met treachery with treachery, and fraud with guile, the civilized settlers were ablaze with indignation for no better reason than that the savages had learned of them, and bettered their instructions.

His Amusements

His Amusements.

"Let your Recreations be Manful, not Sinful."

OF all the amusements of the Colonial Cavalier, none was so popular as gambling. The law strove in vain to break it up. This statute in the Colonial Record, tells its own story: "Against gaming at dice and cardes, be it ordained by this prefent affembly that the winners and loofers fhall forfaicte ten fhillings a man, one ten fhillings thereof to go to the difcoverer, and the reft to pious ufes." I fear very little was ever collected for pious uses. The difficulty lay in the fact that, as every one played, there was no one to act the spy.

This passion for gaming in the colonies was only a reflection of the craze in England. For more than a century after the return of Charles the Second, the rattle of the dice-box, and the shuffling of cards were the most familiar sounds in every London chocolate-house. Young sinners and old spent their fortunes, and misspent their lives, playing for money at Brooke's or Boodle's. When a man fell dead at the door of White's, he was dragged into the hall amid bets as to whether he were dead or alive, and the surgeon's aid was violently opposed, on the ground of unfairness to those betting on the side of death. The Duke of St. Albans, at eighty, too blind to see the cards, went regularly to a gambling-house with an attendant. Lady Castlemaine lost twenty-five thousand pounds in one night's play. General Braddock's sister, having gamed away her fortune at Bath, finished the comedy by hanging herself. When her affectionate brother heard the news, he remarked jocularly, "Poor Fanny, I always thought she would play till she was forced to tuck herself up."

I offer all this testimony to show that our Colonial Cavalier was only the child of his age, when he too shook the dice, and shuffled the cards. Being short of cash, his bets were generally made in tobacco, or, failing that, in flesh and blood. Many a slave found a new master in the morning, because his old master had been unlucky at play the night before.

In a community so absorbed in the excitement of hazard, the lottery of course took deep hold. The first plantation in America was aided by a grand "standing lottery," with a long list of "welcomes, prises and rewards," amounting to more than ten thousand crowns. The declaration sets forth that "all prises, welcomes and rewards drawne wherever they dwell, shall of the treasurer have present pay, and whosoever under one name or poesie payeth three pound in ready money, shall receive six shillings and eight pence, or a silver spoone of that value at his choice."

"The money for the Adventurers is to be paid to Sir Thomas Smith, Knight, and Treasurer for *Virginia*, or such officers as he shall appoint in City or Country, under the common seale of the company for the receit thereof."

The example thus set, was followed whenever the colonies felt a pressure for money. In Virginia a lottery was established to meet the expenses of the French and Indian War—the drawing directed to be "in the Burgesses' Room of the Capital at Williamsburgh at ten in the morning. Prizes current money from £5 to £2000. The lucky numbers to be published in the *Gazette*."

In Maryland, in the eighteenth century, a "Scheme of Lottery is humbly proposed to the Public for Raising the sum of 510 pounds, current money, to be applied towards completeing the Market-House in Baltimore-Town in Baltimore Co., buying two Fire-Engines and a parcel of Leather-Buckets for the use of the said Town, enlarging the present Public Wharf and Building a new one."

THE COLONIAL CAVALIER.

If gambling was a favorite pastime and the lottery a popular excitement, the Cavalier was not a stranger to manlier sports. Of a brave and ardent temper, and a fine physique, he found at once his work and play in the hardy amusements of the chase. He had learned from the Indian to stalk the deer, walking stealthily behind his horse till a good chance offered to shoot close at hand, and lay the unsuspecting deer at his feet. Sometimes, in the bright October weather, the air would be blue with the smoke of the fires built to start the game. Now, in his heavy leather boots, he would start afoot after wild hare, or by the light of the moon, with a band of servants and dogs, he would hunt the 'possum and the coon. This habit of hunting was so universal that the Colonial Cavalier well merited the sarcasm of *The Spectator*, which described the English country gentleman as lying under the curse pronounced in the words of Goliath, "I will give thee to the fowls of the air and to the beasts of the field." Hunting as a sport may not be spiritualizing, but it certainly is not brutalizing, and as much cannot be said for all the sports of that day, in the Southern colonies of America.

The cock-fight and the gouging-match never lacked as eager a throng of spectators, as gathers to-day at a football game; yet both were brutal and disgusting. They roused the amazement of every foreigner, that such things should be tolerated in a civilized country. The gouging-match was simply a fight of the lowest order. Not only were fists freely used, but the test of success was the ability of the stronger bully to gouge out the eye of his adversary. The under man could only save his sight by humiliating himself to cry out, "Kings Cruse!" or "Enough!"

Anbury, who witnessed several of these matches, says: "I have seen a fellow, reckoned a great adept in gouging, who constantly kept the nails of both his thumb and second finger long and pointed; nay, to prevent their breaking or splitting, he hardened them every evening in a candle."

So familiar was this brutal practice that it supplied a Southern orator in after years with a rhetorical climax when, inciting his countrymen to make war on the mercantile interests of Great Britain, he exclaimed: "Commerce is the apple of England's eye. There let us gouge her!"

The cock-fight was scarcely less degrading than the gouging-match. When a fight was announced, the news spread like lightning, and from all over the country people came thronging, some bringing cocks to be entered in the match, but all with money or tobacco to bet on the result. The scene was one of wild excitement. Men and boys cheered on their favorites, and watched with delight, while the furious cocks thrust at each other with their long spurs of cruel steel.

It is pleasant to turn away from such scenes and sports as these, to read of the *Knights of the Golden Horseshoe* riding up into the wild fastnesses of the Blue Ridge Mountains with Governor Spotswood. It was a right knightly expedition, and one of the most picturesque in American history. They wound through the forest, and forded the rivers, and climbed rocky mountains, and took possession of peak after peak in the name of "His Majesty George the Third." Their horses were shod with iron, which was not usual in those days, and on their return, Governor Spotswood presented each of the Cavaliers as a memento of the journey, with a tiny gold horse-shoe, set with jewels, and bearing the legend, "*Sic juvat transcendere montes.*" The thrifty old king disapproved of this extravagance, and left the Governor to pay for the mementoes out of his own pocket.

Riding on horseback was the chief recreation, as well as the chief mode of getting about, at the South. As the planters grew richer, they delighted to own fine horses and outfits. Washington's letter-book contains an order sent to London for elaborate equipments: "1 man's riding saddle, hogskin seat, large plated stirrups, double-reined bridle and Pelham bit plated. A very neat and fashionable Newmarket saddle-cloth. A large and best portmanteau, saddle, bridle and pillion, cloak-bag, and surcingle. A riding-frock of a handsome drab-coloured broadcloth with plain double gilt buttons. A riding waistcoat of superfine scarlet cloth and gold lace, with buttons like those of the coat. A blue surtout coat. A neat switch whip, silver cap. Black velvet cap for servant."

Washington, as methodical in private affairs as in public, kept in his household books, a register of the names and ages of his horses and his dogs. Here we may read the entire family history of *Ajax* and *Blueskin, Valiant* and *Magnolia*, or of the foxhounds *Vulcan, Singer, Ringwood, Music,* and *True Love.*

There was a peculiar intimacy between the foxhounds and their master, for they were associated with some of the happiest hours of his life, and when they came in from a field-day, torn by the briars through which they had struggled or limping from thorns in the foot, they were tenderly cared for, bandaged, and looked after. No amusement so delighted Washington as riding across country with Lord Fairfax in one of the hunts which that gentleman and sportsman was so fond of organizing at Greenaway Court. On a brisk yet soft autumn morning, through the blue Virginia haze, the gentry for miles around came to the "meet." The huntsmen might be heard urging on the dogs with cries of "Yoicks! Yoicks! Have at him! Push him up!" till the fox, which had doubled on its tracks, round and round the thick covert, at length broke away, and the cry was raised of "Tally-ho! Gone away!" The huntsman blew his horn, the whipper-in cracked his whip, the hounds were in full cry, and the entire field of scarlet-coated riders broke in, in a mad gallop, through brush and briar. A strong fox will "live" before hounds on an average of an hour, but sometimes the hunt lasted all day, and covered thirty miles or more. The lessons of endurance, of woodcraft, and of hardy strength, which the Virginia gentlemen learned in these hunts, stood them in good stead in the life-and-death struggle on sterner fields.

A great lover of animals was Charles Lee, who was always surrounded by a troop of dogs, and who made himself somewhat unwelcome as a visitor, by insisting on bringing them into the house with him wherever he went. "I must have some object to embrace," he once wrote to a friend. "When I can be convinced that men are as worthy objects as dogs, I shall transfer my benevolence, and become as staunch a philanthropist as the canting Addison affected to be."

Apparently he never changed his mind, but died

still devoted to his dogs and his horses. Men who loved horses, of course loved horse-racing as well. The Carolina Jockey Club was a famous institution. Its annual races drew crowds from the neighboring country, and the population gave itself up to several days' festivity, ending in a ball. In Virginia, the sport was no less popular. *The Gazette* of October, 1737, announces that "On St. Andrew's Day, there are to be horse-races and several other Diversions for the entertainment of the Gentlemen and Ladies at the Old Field." The programme of this entertainment recalls the days of Merrie England. Besides the race of twenty horses for a prize of five pounds, the advertisement gives notice:

"That a hat of the value of 20s. be cudgelled for, and that after the first challenge be made, the Drums are to beat every quarter of an hour for 3 challenges round the Ring, and none to play with their left hand.

"That a violin be played for by 20 Fiddles, no person to have the liberty of playing unless he bring his fiddle with him. After the prize is won, they are all to play together, and each a different tune, and to be treated by the company.

"That 12 Boys of 12 years of age do run 112 yds, for a hat of the cost of 12 shillings.

"That a flag be flying on said Day, 30 feet high.

"That a handsome entertainment be provided for the subscribers and their wives; and such of them as are not so happy as to have wives, may treat any other lady.

"That drums, trumpets and hautboys be provided to play at said entertainment.

"That after dinner the Royal Health, His Honor the Governor's, etc., are to be drunk.

"That a Quire of Ballads be sung for, by a number of songsters, all of them to have liquor sufficient to clear their wind-pipes.

"That a pair of silver buckles be wrestled for, by a number of brisk young men.

"That a pair of handsome shoes be danced for.

"That a pair of handsome silk stockings, of one pistole value, be given to the handsomest young country maid that appears in the field—with many other whimsical and comical diversions too numerous to mention.

"And as this mirth is designed to be purely innocent and void of offense, all persons resorting there are desired to behave themselves with decency and sobriety."

There is a delightful heartiness and simplicity about all this racing, and chasing, and dancing, and jigging, and fiddling. Folks had not learned to take their pleasure sadly. They still found clowns funny, and shouted with laughter over the efforts to climb greased poles and catch slippery pigs, and, above all, they delighted in the barbecue. At these great open-air feasts animals were roasted whole over enormous fires. Huge bowls of punch circled round the long tables spread under the trees, and when the feast was done the negroes gathered up the fragments and made merry, late into the night.

All the English holidays were observed in the Cavalier Colonies in addition to some local festivals. Eddis writes from Annapolis in old colony days: "Besides our regular assemblies, every mark of attention is paid to the patron saint of each parent dominion; and St. George, St. Andrew, St. Patrick, and St. David are celebrated with every partial mark of national attachment. General invitations are given, and the appearance is always numerous and splendid. The Americans on this part of the continent have likewise a saint, whose history, like those of the above venerable characters, is lost in sable uncertainty. The first of May is, however, set apart to the memory of Saint *Tamina* (Tammany); on which occasion the natives wear a piece of a buck's tail in their hats, or in some conspicuous situation. During the course of the evening, and generally in the midst of a dance, the company are interrupted by the sudden intrusion of a number of persons habited like Indians, who rush violently into the room, singing the war-song, giving the whoop, and dancing in the style of those people; after which ceremony, a collection is made, and they retire, well satisfied with their reception and entertainment."

In addition to such festivities as these, the King's birthnight was celebrated with illuminations and joy-fires, and Christmas in Maryland and Virginia recalled the gayety of the dear old home festival. The halls were filled with holly and mistletoe, which refuse to grow in the chill New England air, but may be gathered in the woods of Virginia as freely as in England; the yule log was kindled on the hospitable hearth, and the evening ended with a dance.

It was a dancing age. None were too old or too dignified to join in the pastime. We have it on the authority of General Greene that on one occasion Washington danced for three hours without once sitting down. Patrick Henry would close the doors of his office to betake himself to dancing or fiddling, and Jefferson dearly loved to rosin his bow for a merry jig. The story is told of him that once, when away from home, he received news of the burning of his father's house. "Did you save any of my books?" he asked of the slave who brought him the tidings. "No, Massa," answered the negro, "but we saved the fiddle!"

THE COLONIAL CAVALIER.

At the entertainments in the "Palace" at Williamsburg, the Governor himself opened the ball, with the most distinguished lady present, in the stately figures of the minuet. Afterward young and old joined in the livelier motions of the *Virginia Reel*. This dance, in spite of its name, did not spring from Virginia soil, but was adopted from an old English dance known as "The Hemp-Dressers," whose figures represent the process of weaving, as its couples shoot from side to side, then over and under, like a shuttle, and finally unite, as the threads tighten and draw the cloth together.

The Governor's palace did not absorb all the gayety of Williamsburg. Who has not heard of the Raleigh Tavern, with its leaden bust of Sir Walter, and its crowning glory of "The Apollo Room," named doubtless for that famous "Apollo Room" in the "Devil's Tavern," Fleet Street, where Shakespeare and Jonson held their bouts of wit and wine?

If we could have crept up to the Raleigh Tavern some night, early in the last half of the last century, and peeped through the small-paned windows of "the Apollo," we might have seen a party of gay collegians making merry with their sweethearts and friends. This tall youth, with sandy hair and gray eyes, is Tom Jefferson, who is offering his awkward homage at the shrine of Miss 'Becca Burwell. Near them is Jefferson's most intimate friend, Jack Page, dancing with his Nancy. Yonder, near the wide fireplace, between Sukey Potter and Betsy Moore, stands Ben Harrison, a mere boy still, though soon to enter the House of Burgesses, and over there in the corner, gravely surveying the dancers, is the uniformed figure of the young soldier, George Washington. Should we have read in these youthful faces a promise of the parts they were destined to play on the world's stage? Probably no more than we should have foreseen this gay ballroom turned into the hall of a political assembly, where the first birth-cry of American freedom is heard.

We can get whatever impression we choose of Williamsburg and its society by selecting our authority judiciously. Burnaby, who visited it in 1759, describes it as a pleasant little town, with wooden houses straggling along unpaved streets; while Hugh Jones writes, thirty years earlier, that many good families live here "who dress after the same modes and behave themselves exactly as the Gentry in London." "Most families of any note," he adds, "have a coach, chariot, Berlin or chaise."

The city, so he says, is well stocked with rich stores, and "at the Governor's House upon Birthnights and at Balls and Assemblies, I have seen as fine an appearance, as good diversion, and as splendid entertainments in Governor Spotswood's time as I have seen anywhere."

When Governor Botetourt (pronounced after the English fashion, *Bottatot*) came over to Virginia, he took the oath of office here at Williamsburg, and rode in state in a great coach drawn by six milk-white horses. After the oath had been administered, a grand supper was given in his honor at the Raleigh Tavern. *The Gazette* gives a full account of the affair. An ode was sung, beginning:

> "He comes! His Excellency comes
>   To cheer Virginia's plains.
> Fill your brisk bowls, ye loyal sons,
>   And sing your loftiest strains!
> Be this your glory, this your boast,
> Lord Botetourt's the favorite toast.
>   Triumphant wreaths entwine!
> Fill your bumpers swiftly round,
> And make your spacious rooms resound
>   With music, joy and wine!"

The air being ended, the recitative took up the strain of effusive compliment:

> "Search every garden, strip the shrubby bowers,
>   And strew his path with sweet autumnal flowers!
> Ye virgins, haste; prepare the fragrant rose
> And with triumphant laurels crown his brows!"

The virgins thus called forth, appeared from their "shrubby bowers," bearing roses and laurel, and singing, as they advanced toward the hero of the evening:

> "See, we've stripped each flowery bed—
> Here's laurels for his lordly head,
> And while Virginia is his care,
> May he protect the virtuous fair!"

As I looked on Lord Botetourt's statue, and marked its moss-covered figure and its fatuously smiling face, robbed of its nose by the stone of contempt, I remembered this festival, and mused on the vicissitudes of fame.

In the year 1752 a new delight was opened to the provincials. Hallam's company of comedians came over in *The Charming Sally* to act for them. A playbill of that year announces that "at the new theatre in Annapolis by the company of comedians, on Monday next, being the sixth of this instant July, will be performed *The Busy Body*, likewise a farce called *The Lying Valet*. To begin precisely at 7 o'clock. Tickets to be had at the printing-office. No persons to be admitted behind the scenes. Box seats 10s., pit 7s. 6d, gallery 5s." A later bill announces that "children in laps will not be admitted."

The favorite plays given by Hallam's Company seem to have been—

"The Suspicious Husband," "Othello," "The Mock Doctor," "Romeo and Juliet," "The Devil To Pay," "A Bold Stroke for a Wife," and "Miss In Her Teens; or, A Medley of Lovers."

Our squeamish age would find much to shock, and perhaps little to amuse, in many of those old plays. Congreve's shameless muse set the pace, and the Nell Gwynns of the stage kept it. If we wonder that our ancestors could listen and look, will not our descendants wonder equally at us?

Before Hallam and his company came over to set up a professional standard, amateur theatricals were the rage. The Virginia *Gazette* in 1736 announces a performance of "*The Beaux' Stratagem* by the gentlemen and ladies of this county," and also that the students of the college are to give *The Tragedy of Cato* at the theatre. Somehow, Addison's tragedies seem further removed from our sympathies than Congreve's comedies, and we turn with relief to a form of amusement always in fashion and forever modern, the time-honored entertainment of feasting.

In 1744, a grand dinner was given by Governor Gooch to visiting statesmen at Annapolis. William Black, who was present, records in his journal that "Punch was served before dinner, which was sumptuous, with wines in great abundance, followed by strawberries and ice-cream, a great rarity." These public banquets were momentous affairs, demanding a sound digestion and a steady head in those guests who wished to live to dine another day. Chastellux gives a vivid account of their customs. "The dinner," he writes, "is served in the American or, if you will, in the English fashion, consisting of two courses, one comprehending the entrées, the roast meat and the warm side-dishes; the other, the sweet pastry and confectionery. When this is removed, the cloth is taken off, and apples, nuts, and chestnuts are served. It is then that healths are drunk." This custom of drinking healths, he finds pleasant enough, inasmuch as it serves to stimulate and prolong conversation. But he says, "I find it an absurd and truly barbarous practice, the first time you drink, and at the beginning of the dinner, to call out successively to each individual, to let him know you drink his health. The actor in this ridiculous comedy is sometimes ready to die with thirst, whilst he is obliged to inquire the names, or catch the eyes, of twenty-five or thirty persons."

The woes of the diner and winer do not, it seems, end with this general call, for he is constantly called, and having his sleeve pulled, to attract his attention, now this way, now that. "These general and partial attacks end in downright duels. They call to you from one end of the table to the other: 'Sir, will you permit me to drink a glass of wine with you?'"

Allowing for some exaggeration on the part of the lively Frenchman, it is easy to see what quantities of Madeira and "Phyall" must have been drunk in those tournaments of courtesy, and I do not wonder to read in the journal of a young woman of the eighteenth century: "The gentlemen are returned from dinner. Both tipsy!"

"The Tuesday Club," of Maryland, had many a jovial supper together. Their toasts always began with "The Ladies," followed by "The King's Majesty," and after that "The Deluge." I find a suggestive regulation made by this club, that each member should bring his own sand-box, "to save the carpet."

Parson Bacon sanctified these convivial meetings by his presence and was, by all accounts, the ringleader of the boisterous revels. Jonathan Boucher, another clergyman, but of a very different type, was a great clubman too. He was one of the leading spirits of "The Hommony Club," whose avowed object was "to promote innocent mirth and ingenious humor."

The days of women's clubs were still in the far future, and the chief excitement of the ladies was an occasional ball. The Maryland assemblies began at six o'clock in the evening, and were supposed to end at ten, though the young folks often coaxed and cajoled the authorities into later hours. Card parties were part of the entertainment, and whist was enlivened by playing for money. The supper was often furnished from the ladies' kitchens and the gentlemen's gamebags, and was a tempting one. The costumes were rich and imposing. A witness of one of these Maryland balls writes: "The gentlemen, dressed in short breeches, wore handsome knee-buckles, silk stockings, buckled pumps, etc. The ladies wore—God knows what; I don't!"

Dancing and music were the chief branches of the eighteenth-century maiden's education. I can fancy, as I read that "Patsy Custis and Milly Posey are gone to Colonel Mason's to the dancing-school," how they held up their full petticoats, and pointed out the toes of their red-heeled shoes, and dreamed of future conquests, although for one of them the tomb was already preparing its chill embrace.

For women, life in town was pleasant enough with its tea-drinkings, its afternoon visits, and its evening assemblies, but on the plantations far from neighbors time must often have hung heavy on their hands. Yet even there, pleasures could be found, or made. When evening shut down over the lonely manor-houses along the Chesapeake, the myrtleberry candles were lighted, the slender-legged mahogany tables drawn out, and the Colonial dames seated themselves to an evening of cards. Small stakes were played for to heighten the interest of "Triumph, Ruff and Honors," "Gleke," or "Quadrille;" and when these lost their charm, there was the spinet to turn to.

Spinet.

In those primitive days people still loved melody. "A little music" was called for with enthusiasm, and given without hesitation. There was no scientific criticism to be feared when the young men and maidens "raised a tune." Their list of songs was not long; but familiarity lent a deeper charm than novelty. "Gaze not on Swans" was a favorite in the seventeenth century. "Push about the Brisk Bowl," while well enough at the hunt supper table, was banished from the drawing-room in favor of "Beauty, Retire!" a song beginning—

> "Beauty, retire! thou dost my pitty move;
> Believe my pitty and then trust my love."

The writer does not make it quite clear why he wishes Beauty to retire, nor why she moves his pity. In fact, the case seems quite reversed in the last stanza:

> "With niew and painfulle arts
> Of studied warr I breake the hearts
> Of half the world; and shee breakes mine;
> And shee, and shee, and *shee* breakes mine!"

Through the lapse of more than one century, we hear the echo of those young voices, rising and falling in the air and counter of the quaint old melodies.

Oh, those shadowy corners of candle-lighted rooms, those spinets, those duos and trios, those ruffled squires and brocaded dames!—where are they now?

His Man-Servants and His Maid-Servants

His Man-Servants and his Maid Servants.

"JOVE fixed it certain
That whatever day
Makes a man slave,
Takes half his worth away"

A NEW ENGLAND farmhouse and a Southern plantation:—What a contrast the two presented in colonial days! In the homes of Massachusetts and Connecticut, the notable housewife was up before light, breaking the ice over the water, of a winter morning, preparing with her own hands the savory sausages and buckwheat cakes for the men's breakfast, and setting the house in order. To her it fell to take charge of the wool from the back of the sheep till it reached the back of her boy; carding, spinning, weaving, dyeing the wool, cutting the cloth, and sewing the seams, scouring floors and washing dishes; all these duties fell to the share of the Puritan Priscillas. Yet, when evening fell, when the dishes were shelved on the dresser, these busy housewives, in their sanded kitchens, with the firelight reflected from their shining tins, were not to be pitied, even in comparison with their more luxuriously attended sisters in Maryland or Virginia.

Life at the South was at once grander and shabbier, than in New England. The Southerner's ease-loving nature had the power to ignore detail; and it is attention to detail which brings well-being to the household and wrinkles to the housekeeper. A thousand slaves could not take the place of one woman of "faculty." In fact, the more shiftless, lazy negroes there were, the less order and tidiness prevailed. But order and tidiness were not indispensable to happiness there and then, and the sum of human enjoyment was large on those old plantations, in spite of shiftlessness and slavery. Of that restless ambition which corrodes modern life, men had little, women had none, and servants less than none. The negro was a true child of the tropics, and with food and sunshine enough, was merry as the day is long.

A healthy negro, on a prosperous estate, under the charge of a gentleman, not under the bane of an overseer, came perhaps as near to animal cheerfulness as mortal often does. The master enjoyed that serenity and leisure which freedom from manual labor gives; his children grew up, each with a personal retainer attached to himself with the old feudal loyalty; the lady of the house was again the old Saxon *hlaefdige*, who gave out the bread to the tribe of servants day by day. Yet with all the brightness which can be thrown into the picture, slavery was a curse alike to slave and slave-owner, on account both of what it brought and what it took away.

It is strange to note how silently and unperceived the black cloud of slavery stole over the Colonial Cavalier. A casual entry in John Rolfe's journal records: "About the last of August came in a dutch man of warre that sold vs twenty Negars." Before the arrival of this fatal vessel life-servitude was unknown. The system of apprenticeship, and what would now be called contract labor, prevailed. These indented white servants were either transported convicts, sold for a season to the planters, or, like the Maryland *redemptioners*, poor immigrants, who contracted to serve for a period of time equivalent to the cost of their passage, which was prepaid to the master of the ship on which they came.

The work of these indented servants was not excessive. "Five dayes and a halfe in the summer," said one who knew the situation from experience, "is the allotted time that they worke and, for two months, when the sun predominates in the highest pitch of his heat, they claim an antient and customary Priviledge, to repose themselves three hours in the day, within the house. In Winter they do little but hunt and build fires."

The Sot-Weed Factor gives a much less rose-colored account of the life of a redemptioner. A woman-servant in the poem, looking back on her life in England, exclaims:

> "Not then a slave for twice two year,
> My cloathes were fashionably new,
> Nor were my shifts of linnen blue.
> But things are changed: Now at the Hoe
> I daily work and Barefoot go,
> In weeding corn, or feeding Swine
> I spend my melancholy time."

A "melancholy time" many of the redemptioners must have had in their enforced service; but if the master proved too severe, the indented servant had the privilege of selecting another, and the original employer was indemnified for his loss. Susan Frizell, who had run away from her master, was recaptured and brought before the court for punishment; but her accounts of ill-usage so moved the authorities, that they remitted the extra term of service to which running away had made her liable, and only demanded that she should earn under a new master the five hundred pounds of tobacco to be paid to her old employer. The bystanders were so touched by poor Susan's pitiful situation that they collected six hundred pounds on the spot, and sent Susan on her way rejoicing, with a capital of one hundred pounds of tobacco to give her a new start in the world.

The law provided that the servant, when his time of service expired, should receive a portion of goods sufficient to make him an independent freeman, who might rise to be a councillor or an assemblyman. A Colonial statute directs that "at the end of said terme of service, the master or mistress of such servant shall give unto such man or maid-servant, 3 barrels, a hilling hoe and a felling axe; and to a man-servant, one new cloth suite, one new shirte, 1 new paire shoes, and a new Monmouth capp; and to a maid-servant, 1 new pettycoat and waistcoat, 1 new smock, 1 pair new shoes, 1 pair new stockings and the cloaths formerly belonging to the servant."

The advantage of this system of indented service lay in its gradual absorption of the immigrant population, who thus had time to understand the laws and institutions of their new country before they became in their turn citizens and lawmakers. The disadvantage lay in the encouragement it gave to kidnapping. Many children and young people in the seaboard towns of England were beguiled, or carried by force, on shipboard, to be sold as servants in the colonies. The kidnappers, or "spirits," as they were commonly called, served as bugaboos in many an English nursery to frighten naughty children into obedience under threat of being spirited away to America.

Howells' "State-Trials" contains a pitiful account of the experiences of a young nobleman sold as a white servant in Virginia through the plot of his covetous uncle, who wanted his property. The nephew is a mere child when he begins his apprenticeship in the provinces, but, by a series of attempts to escape, he prolongs his term of service till, when he finally succeeds in getting back to England to claim his own from the treacherous uncle, he is a man grown, and as difficult of recognition as the Tichborne claimant. The great majority of the first indented servants sent over, however, were convicts ripe for the jail or the gallows, and only respited to be transported to the colonies, which long suffered from the introduction of such a class of citizens.

The records of Middlesex County, England, tell their own story:

3 *April*, 15 *James I.*

Stephen Rogers, for killing George Watkins against the form of Statute of the first year of King James, convicted of manslaughter, was sentenced to be hung, but at the instance of Sir Thomas Smith, Kn't, was reprieved in the interest of Virginia, because he was a carpenter.

6 *August, 16 James I.*

On his conviction of incorrigible vagabondage Ralph Rookes was reprieved at Sheriff Johnson's order so that he should be sent to Virginia.

28 *April, 18 James I.*

On her conviction by a Jury of stealing divers goods of Mary Payne, Elizabeth Handsley was reprieved for Virginia.

31*st May, 18 James I.*

On his conviction of stealing Richard Atkinson's bull, William Hill asked for the book, and was respited, for Virginia.

The records teem with such cases. Yet these were not the only representatives of indented servants. In the course of the various successive political upheavals which shook England, it chanced that many gentlemen of good birth and breeding were driven over to the colonies, to begin life there at the foot of the ladder. After Monmouth's Rebellion several hundred citizens, some of eminent standing, were sent to Virginia. "Take care," wrote the king, "that they continue to serve for ten years at least, and that they be not permitted in any manner to redeem themselves by money or otherwise, until that term be fully expired." Despite the royal warning, these exiles were pardoned before the term was ended, and became most useful and valuable citizens.

Well had it been for the Cavalier colonies had they adhered to this system of apprenticeship and indented service. Their children and their children's children might then have sung of "the nobility of labor, the long pedigree of toil." But with the widespread introduction of negro slavery, came the degradation of labor. The negro represented a despised caste. He labored; therefore labor was contemptible. Henceforth there was established an aristocracy of ease and wealth, resting on a foundation of unpaid labor.

With the establishment of slavery there grew up a more marked distinction of classes among the whites. A wide gulf separated rich and poor. Devereux Jarratt, son of a Virginia carpenter, writes in his autobiography: "We were accustomed to look upon gentlefolks as beings of a superior order. For my part, I was quite shy of them and kept off a humble distance. A periwig in those days was a distinguishing badge of gentlefolk; and when I saw a man riding the road with a wig on, it would so alarm my fears, and give me such a disagreeable feeling, that I dare say I would run as for my life."

Thus society became stratified: At the top, the great landholders, below them the small planters aping the manners and customs of their rich neighbors, and underneath, the population composed of poor whites and overseers. The negroes were no more part of the social system than the oxen they drove a-field.

It is a curious commentary on the Scriptural principle of turning the other cheek to the smiter, that the Indians, who resisted the encroachments of the whites and waved the tomahawk in response to the echo of the Englishman's gun, were feared and respected, while the blacks, who yielded meekly to the yoke of servitude, met at best only a good-natured contempt.

The masters' consciousness of the injustice of slavery made them fearful of revolt and revenge, which the slaves had neither skill nor energy to plan. The whole machinery of the law was directed to the suppression of this imaginary danger. All gatherings of slaves were strictly forbidden. If found at a distance from the plantations, any negro was subject to lashes on the bare back. It was not counted a felony to kill a slave while punishing him. Negroes, and indented servants as well, who attempted to escape were whipped and branded on the cheek with the letter R, and on a repetition of the offence they might be put to death. No punishment was too severe for this crime of running away, curiously denominated in the old statutes "stealth of one's self." Among the enormous offences set forth in a Maryland Act of 1638 I find, "Harboring or clokeing of another's servant without the knowledge and consent of the Master or Mistress."

In spite of all precautions, a slave did succeed, now and then, in gaining his freedom. It is with great satisfaction that I read an old Act of Assembly, setting forth that "Whereas a negro named Billy, slave to John Tillit, has for several years unlawfully absented himself from his master's service, said Billy is pronounced an outlaw, and a bounty of a thousand pounds of tobacco set on his head." The bounty does not trouble me, for I feel sure that the craft and strength which made Billy an outlaw, kept him safe from the bolts aimed against him by the colonial legislature.

The statute-books of Maryland and Virginia are records of the barbarity into which injustice may drive a kindly, liberty-loving people who are forced into cruelty by the logic of events. Having taken the wrong road, like Bunyan's Pilgrim, the Cavaliers found the rocks ready to fall on them if they went forward, and the gulf yawning behind them if they tried to turn back.

It must never be forgotten in their behalf that they did try to turn about, when they saw their error. Their best men, over and over again, urged the prohibiting of slavery, and there is more than a probability that they would have won their cause, but for the attitude of that country whose air was afterward pronounced too pure to be breathed by a slave insomuch that his shackles fell off, when he touched the shore sacred to liberty. Yet, in 1695, this highly moral and philanthropic England declared in a statute, the opinion of its king and Parliament, that the slave-trade was highly beneficial to the kingdom and colonies. In 1712, Queen Anne boasted in her speech to Parliament, of her success in securing to England a new market for slaves in Spanish America. Jefferson testified that Virginia was constantly balked in her efforts to throw off slavery by the attitude of the home government. Carolina attempted restriction and gained a rebuke. In 1775, the Earl of Dartmouth haughtily replied to a colonial agent, "We cannot allow the colonies to check, or discourage in any degree, a traffic so beneficial to the nation."

Yet all the blame cannot be thrown on England. Had the colonies been as firm in defence of their duties, as they were when their rights were in question, England must have yielded. Virginia was the first State to enunciate the proposition of the equality of man, yet was blind to her own inconsistency. The leading supporters of the cause of liberty were themselves slave-owners. George Washington owned negroes. John Randolph had a bunk for his slave side by side with the bed of his pet horse. Patrick Henry wrote with admirable candor: " Believe me, I shall honor the Quakers for their noble efforts to abolish slavery; they are equally calculated to promote moral and political good. Would any one believe that I am master of slaves of my own purchase? I am drawn along by the general inconvenience of living without them. I will not—I *can* not—justify it." The great Southern statesman said that he trembled for his country when he remembered that God was just. Washington deplored the system, yet so closely were all commercial and political interests interwoven with it that it seemed impossible to disentangle them. Even philanthropy did not scorn its alliance. Whitefield expended the money raised by his eloquent preaching at Charleston, on a plantation with slaves to work it for the benefit of an orphan asylum.

The Church spread its surplice of protection over the institution. Baptism was permitted to the slave, but with the distinct understanding that it was to make no difference in the condition of bondage of these brothers in Christ. One South Carolina clergyman ventured to preach on the duties of masters to their servants, but his congregation said to him: "Sir, we pay you a genteel salary to read to us the prayers of the liturgy and to explain to us such parts of the Gospel as the rule of the Church directs, but we do not want you to teach us what to do with our blacks."

The Northern colonies were freed from the curse of slaveholding as much by policy as by principle. They tried slave-owning, but, happily for them, it did not pay. The climate and the conditions of their industries forbade its spread among them. But their hands were not unstained. If they did not buy slaves, they sold them. There still exists, if Bishop Meade may be trusted, a bill of sale of a slave, bearing the signature of Jonathan Edwards.

Every year ships were fitted out from Medford, Salem, or New Bedford, which sailed away loaded with rum to be exchanged in Africa for negroes, who in turn were sold for molasses, to be made into rum again. The transactions of one of these slavers are preserved in the History of Medford, and makes interesting reading for those who would hold up the Puritan as innocent of the transgression which stains the character of the Cavalier. The deadly parallel column tells its story, so that he who runs may read:

Dr. The Natives of Annamboe.	Per Contra. Cr.
1770. Gals	1770. Gals
Apr. 22. To 1 hh. of rum..... 110	Apr. 22. By 1 Woman Slave......... 110
May 1. " " " 130	May 1. By 1 Prime Woman Slave. 130
May 2. " " " 105	May 2. By 1 Boy Slave 4 ft. 1 in..... 105
May 7. " " " 130	May 7. By 1 Boy Slave 4 ft. 3 in.... 108
May 5. Cash in gold 5 oz... 2	May 5. 1 Prime Man Slave 5 oz..... 2
" 5. " " " 2 oz. " 5. 2 doz. of snuff 1 oz. } 3	May 5. 1 Old Man for a Lingister... 3 oz

The negroes thus brought to the American colonies were not of one race. A slaver often carried men of different languages, habits, and characteristics, perhaps hereditary enemies. Some were jet black, some mahogany-colored, and others still of a tawny yellow, with flat noses and projecting jaws. This last type belonged to the low, swampy ground at the Niger's delta, and marked the race most adapted to the cultivation of the rice in its swamps, so fatal to white laborers. All this diversity among the negroes accounts for their lack of power and energy to combine in a struggle for freedom. "The negroes that have been slaves in their own country," Hugh Jones says, "make the best servants; for they that have been kings and great men there, are generally lazy, haughty and obstinate." Alas, for these poor magnates from Heathendom!

THE COLONIAL CAVALIER.

The Cavaliers did not find the problem of domestic service solved by life-ownership of servants. Colonel Fitzhugh writes Mr. John Buckner in 1680: "I hope you will make an abatement for your Dumb Negro that you sold me. Had she been a new Negro, I must have blamed my fate, not you; but one that you had two years, I must conclude you knew her qualities, which is *bad at work, worse at talking.* You took advantage of the softness of my messenger to quit your hands of her."

In spite of this unsuccessful experiment, we find him two years later making another venture in human live-stock, by ordering John Withers to buy "Mr. Walton's Boy for £20, or £54 with him and 2 others, unlesse you can make a better bargain." Poor Colonel Fitzhugh might well be discouraged, for he had tried every kind of servant, black and white, bond and free, without satisfactory results. "I would have you," he writes in despair to a sea captain in England, "bring me in a good housewife. I do not intend or mean to be brought in, as the ordinary servants are, but to pay her passage and agree to give her fifty shillings or three pounds a year during the space of five years, upon which terms, I suppose, good servants may be had, because they have their passage clear, and as much money as they can have there. *I would have a good one or none.* I look upon the generality of wenches you bring in as not worth keeping."

So the Colonial Cavaliers found trouble in their households with servants of any race or color, and the gentle nature of the blacks proving specially adaptable to servitude, and purchase money seeming so much less than wage-money, they gradually did away with other service. Every plantation had its negro-quarters, where crowds of pickaninnies swarmed in the sunshine outside the little cabins with scarcely more clothing on than their parents had worn in their African jungle. The bread of Indian corn was baked on the hoe over a smoky fire, or in the ashes. When the day's work was done, the negroes sat, with their banjos or rude musical instruments, playing accompaniments to their strange, weird music, a mixture of reminiscences of barbarism and the hymns they caught from the "New Lights"; or they spent the evening more merrily, dancing jigs to the twanging of a broken fiddle. They were, on the whole, a careless, happy race, taking no thought for the morrow, content to accept food and clothing at the hands of "Massa and Missus," and, for the rest, to work when they must, shirk when they could, and carry a merry heart through life. The outward circumstances of their lot were hard. Anbury, in his American travels, observed their condition closely and described it with what we must believe impartial accuracy. The life of these field-hands was much more severe than that of the household servants, both because the work itself was harder, and because it was ruled by the overseer, usually a brute. It is of these field negroes that Anbury is writing, when he says: "They are called up at daybreak, and seldom allowed to swallow a mouthful of hominy or hoecake, but are driven out into the field immediately, where they continue at hard labor without intermission till noon, when they go to their dinners and are seldom allowed an hour for that purpose. Their meals consist of hominy and salt, and if their master is a man of humanity, touched by the finer feelings of love and sensibility, he allows them twice a week a little fat, skimmed milk, rusty bacon or salt herring to relish this miserable and scanty fare. . . . After they have dined they return to labor in the field till dusk in the evening. Here one naturally imagines the daily labor of these poor creatures over; not so. They repair to the tobacco-houses, where each has a task of *stripping* allotted, which takes up some hours; or else they have such a quantity of Indian corn to husk, and if they neglect it, are tied up in the morning, and receive a number of lashes from those unfeeling monsters, the overseers. When they lay themselves down to rest, their comforts are equally miserable and limited, for they sleep on a bench, or on the ground with an old scanty blanket, which serves them at once for bed and covering. Their clothing is not less wretched, consisting of a shirt and trousers of coarse, thin, hard, hempen stuff in the Summer, with an addition of a very coarse woolen jacket, breeches, and shoes in Winter." Yet, in spite of toil and privation, these negroes, so the traveller testifies, are jovial and contented.

It seems incomprehensible to us that the noble, sensitive, kindly Southern gentleman saw all these things in silence; that even when they had no share in the beating of the wayfarer, they still passed by on the other side with the priest or the Levite and offered no succor. Yet, do we not do the same thing every day? We know that the faces of the poor are ground while the rich prosper, that the animal world is abused and tortured, yet because we think ourselves powerless, we strive to make ourselves callous, and turn away our eyes that we may not see where we cannot help.

Many there were who had the courage as well as the impulse to protest. One of the firmest and the ablest of these was Jefferson. He had the insight to perceive not only the injustice to the slave, but the injury to the slaveholder. "There must, doubtless," he writes, "be an unhappy influence on the manners of our people by the existence of slavery among us. The whole commerce between master and slave is a perpetual exercise of the most boisterous passions, the most unremitting despotism on the one part, and degrading submission on the other. Our children see this and learn to imitate it, for man is an imitative animal. This quality is the germ of all education in him. From his cradle to his grave, he is learning to do what he sees others do. If a parent could find no motive either in his philanthropy or his self-love for restraining the intemperance of passion toward his slave, it should always be a sufficient one that his child is present. But generally it is not sufficient. The parent storms; the child looks on, catches the lineaments of wrath, puts on the same airs in the circle of smaller slaves, gives a loose to the worst of his passions; and thus nursed, educated, and daily exercised in tyranny, cannot but be stamped by it with odious peculiarities. The man must be a prodigy who can retain his manners and morals undepraved by such circumstances."

Yet we are constantly meeting such prodigies in the history of the Cavalier. Men whose pure lives, gentle manners, and courtesy to high and low, whose unselfishness and cheerful benignity may be matched against those of the hardest-working Puritan or the most radical upholder of the equal rights of man. The old *noblesse oblige* principle still held sway. Governor Gouch, of Virginia, being once on a time reproached for having returned the bow of a negro, replied in the good old Cavalier spirit: "I should be much ashamed that a negro should have better manners than I." The field hands were kept at a distance, but the house-servants were admitted to the closest intimacy, especially when acting in the capacity of maids and nurses. Many a golden head was laid for comfort on the black breast of some faithful Mammy, while the childish sorrows were poured into her listening ear, and many a gray-haired woman recalled as her truest friend, the humble slave whose life had been devoted to her service.

An entry in Washington's journal shows how well he understood the nature of the negro, and how wisely and firmly he dealt with it. One day four of his servants were employed at carpentering, but without accomplishing anything. Instead of scolding, Washington sat himself calmly down to watch their work. Stimulated by his presence, they went on briskly. The wise master noted the work and the time, and then informed them that just so much must be done in his absence. It was owing to such management that the products of the Mount Vernon plantation ranked so high that all barrels marked with the name of George Washington passed the inspectors without examination.

Here, if anywhere, was a man who might be trusted with arbitrary power over his fellow-men, yet he was one of the most outspoken in opposition to slavery; and he, like Jefferson, realized the terrible strain on the character of the master. Woe to the man who lives constantly with inferiors! He is doomed never to hear himself contradicted, never to be told unwelcome truth, never to sharpen his wits and learn to control his temper by argument with equals. The Colonial Cavaliers were little kings, and they proved the truth of the saying of the royal sage of Rome, that the most difficult of tasks is to lead life well in a palace.

His Church

His Church.

Williamsburg Church
Bruton Parish.

"*MIXE not holy thinges with profane!*" so runs the inscription on the quaint old silver chalice used in the communion service of the Jamestown church.

Had the advice been heeded, the history of the Colonial Church of England would not have been the sorry story it is. In point of fact, holy and profane things are so mixed in its chronicles that it is hard to write of it without seeming levity and flippancy. To call the differences between the parsons and their parishes in the Southern Colonies a struggle, would be to dignify it beyond the warrant of truth. It was simply a series of squabbles without ennobling principle on either side. Yet, in the beginning, better things promised. Great attention was paid to religious forms and observances, and the earliest laws are devoted to the regulation of church affairs.

In the year after the landing of the settlers, Edward Maria Wingfield, first president of the council in Virginia, was brought to trial accused of various high crimes and misdemeanors. Among the charges against him was one of atheism. The most damaging evidence against him was the absence of a Bible from his belongings. He himself felt that this was a point needing explanation, which he made by saying that he had "sorted" many books to take with him to Virginia, and was sure that a Bible was among them, but that in the course of his journey he had found "the truncke" somehow broken open, and the Bible "ymbeasiled."

In rebuttal of evidence showing general godlessness and lack of respect for the Sabbath, he explained that on the Sunday in question, Indian allarums had detained every one at the palisade "till the daie was farre spent." Then, he goes on to say: "the preacher, Master Hunt, did aske

me if it weare my pleasure to have a sermon. He
said he was prepared for it. I made answer that
our men were weary and hungry, and that if it
pleased him wee would spare him till some other
tyme."

The tact of this reply should certainly have
scored a point in Wingfield's defence, especially
as he adds: "I never failed to take such noates by
wrighting out of his doctrine as my capacity could
comprehend, *unless some raynie day hindered my endeavour.*"

These excuses, however, were not satisfactory
to his judges, and the other charges against him
proving only too well-founded, he was deposed
from the council, and was glad enough to slip off
back to England at the first chance. Three years
later, Dale of the iron hand came over fresh from
the Netherlands, and put religion, like everything
else, under martial law. The captain of the watch
was made a sort of tithing-man, whose business it
was to preserve order and encourage godliness at
the point of the bayonet. It was his duty, half
an hour before divine service, morning and evening, to shut the ports and place sentinels, and, the
bell having tolled for the last time, to search all
the houses, and to command every one (with the
exception of the sick and hurt) to go to church.
This done, he followed the guards with their arms

into the church, where he laid the keys before the governor. On Sunday he was ordered to see that the day was noways profaned by any disorders.

The Ancient Planters were strict Sunday keepers. The earliest law decrees "The Sabbath to be kept holy, that no journeys be made except in case of emergent necessitie on that day, that no goods bee laden in boates, nor shooteing in gunns or the like tending to the prophanation of the day." The offender who disobeys this decree is sentenced to pay a fine of a hundred pounds of tobacco or "be layd in the stocks."

Henry Coleman was excommunicated for forty days for scornful speeches, and putting on his hat in church. The minister as well as the church was protected by law from irreverence and disrespect. In 1653, it was ordered by the court that, for slandering Rev. Mr. Cotton, "Henry Charlton make a pair of stocks and set in them several Sabbath-days during divine service, and then ask Mr. Cotton's forgiveness for using offensive and slanderous words concerning him." A few years later, Mary Powell, for slandering a minister, was sentenced to receive twenty lashes on her bare shoulders, and to be banished the country. I tremble to think what would have been the fate, had he fallen into episcopal hands, of the Puritan who spoke of bishops as "proud, popish, presumptuous, paltry, pestilent, and pernicious prelates," and further as "impudent, shameless, and *wainscot-faced.*" I, for one, should have voted to take something from his punishment, on the ground of his supplying the world with a new and most expressive phrase.

Maryland, liberal in all sectarian matters, strictly forbade calling names such as "Heretick, Schismatick, Idolator, Papist, Antinomian, etc.," and sentenced the offender to a fine of ten shillings. She also dealt summarily with unbelievers. Her assembly ordained that "whatsoever person or persons shall deny the Holy Trinity, or shall utter reproachful speeches concerning the Trinity or any of the said persons thereof, shall be punished with death and confiscation of land and goods to the Lord Proprietary."

The first church in America was a very simple affair, an old rotten tent set up in the Jamestown marsh under the pines and hemlocks. The soft May weather made even so much shelter unnecessary, and it was replaced by an awning stretched between the rustling boughs. But busy as the settlers were, they set to work at once on a chapel built of logs and covered with sedge and dirt, which in turn was replaced by a church of timber, fifty feet long, by more than twenty in breadth. This finally was replaced by the brick building whose ruined arches alone remain to tell its story.

When Lord De la Warre arrived in Virginia and found the colonists in desperate straits, he wisely occupied their attention by setting them to repair and refurnish the wooden church then in existence, and to decorate it with flowers. Here during his government he worshipped in a degree of state more fitting for a cathedral than for a wooden chapel in the wilderness. He went to church in full dress, attended by his lieutenant-general, admiral, vice-admiral, master of the horse and the rest of the council, with a guard of fifty halberd-bearers in red cloaks behind him. When the service ended, the procession filed out with as much solemnity as it had entered, and escorted the Governor to his house.

Religious observances played an important part in the early days of the settlement. The first statute made by an early legislative assembly, requires that in every plantation some house or room be specially dedicated to the worship of God, sequestered and set apart for that purpose, and not to be of any temporal use whatever.

It is curious, in view of this last clause, to find it recorded of the House of Burgesses itself: "The most convenient place wee could finde to site in was the quire of the churche." Surely no place could have been more appropriate for the gathering of the first free assembly of the people in America, and it was equally fitting that their proceedings should open with a prayer for guidance in the path which was destined to be darker and more difficult than they knew. "Forasmuch as men's affaires doe little prosper when God's service is neglected," a prayer was said by Mr. Bucke, the minister, "that it would please God to guide and sanctifie all our proceedings to His owne glory and the good of this Plantation."

If the church of that time was devoted to temporal uses, religious services were not confined within its walls. Alexander Whitaker, the apostle of Virginia, writes home that he *exercises* at the house of the governor, Sir Thomas Dale, every Saturday night. This "exercising," or hearing of the catechism, with prayer and song, in private houses, was a matter of necessity in days when a parish covered a space hardly to be crossed in a day's journey, with the roads or bridle-paths choked with undergrowth, and blocked by fallen logs. The Rev. Mr. Forbes seems to have been of a complaining nature, yet he rouses one's sympathy when he tells of the difficulties under which he labored.

"My parish," he says, "extendeth LX miles in length, in breadth about XI." Over this distance were scattered some four hundred families, to whom he was expected to minister. "Sometimes," he goes on plaintively, " after I have travelled Fifty Miles to Preach at a Private House, the weather happening to prove bad on the day of our meeting so that very few met, or else being hindred by Rivers and Swamps rendred impassable with much rain, I have returned with doing of nothing to their benefit or mine own satisfaction."

Few clergymen of that day and region took their duties so seriously. They were for the most part quite willing to have service read by some deputy-priest or layman in the " chapels of ease;" or if they must officiate, they chose some sermon from Thomas Fuller or Jeremy Taylor, or, as a last resort, constructed one at small expense of labor on a scaffolding of headings resting on an underpinning of text. A fine example of this method of sermon-building I find in the discourse sent home by the pious Whitaker. He takes as his text, "Cast thy bread upon the waters," and expounds it after this fashion:

" 1. The dutie to be performed: *Cast thy bread.* Be liberal to all.

" 2. The manner of bestowing alms: By *casting* it away.

" 3. What is to be given? *Bread;* all things needful, yes, and of the best kind.

"4. Who may be liberal? Even those that have it. It must be *thy* bread—thine own.

"5. To whom we must be liberal: To all; yea to the *Waters*."

This kind of sermon had the double advantage of being easy for the preacher, and restful to the congregation. It went along at a comfortable jog-trot, like a family horse, and the hearer was in no danger of being hurled over the head of revival eloquence into lurid threats of future punishment. If the preachers of the Church of England did not kindle spiritual ardor, at least they did not keep children awake o' nights, nor frighten nervous women into hysterics.

While these drowsy discourses were going on in the Southern colonies, the Puritan divine in the New England pulpit was throwing off such cheerful observations as these: "Every natural man and woman is born full of all sin, as full as a toad is of poison, as full as ever his skin can hold; mind, will, eyes, mouth; every limb of his body and every piece of his mind." The future awaiting such a wretch, he sets forth vividly: "Thou canst not endure the torments of a little kitchen-fire on the tip of thy finger, not one-half hour together. How wilt thou bear the fury of this infinite, endless, consuming fire in body and soul!" To these inspiring doctrines of the Rev. Thomas Shepherd, another Puritan preacher added his conviction that "there are infants in hell not a span long."

To the credit of the Colonial Church of England be it recorded that no such sentiments disgraced its pulpit and made its Sabbath terrible to little children. The day was one of innocent enjoyment, and the church building was dear to generation after generation, as a peaceful and memory-hallowed spot. The early settlers had little money to spend in adorning their churches, yet from the beginning there was a great difference between the bare and square wooden New England meeting-house and the quaint Southern church of brick or stone, recalling in every line the beloved parish churches of Old England. The churchmen, unlike the Puritans, found no sin in beauty or adornment. St. John's Church at Hampton bore the royal arms carved on its steeple. Colonel Springer left by his will one thousand pounds of tobacco to pay for having the Lord's Prayer and Commandments put up in the new church at Northampton. By a statute of 1660, parishes are enjoined to provide at their own cost a great church Bible and two books of Common Prayer in folio for the minister and "clark"; also communion-plate, pulpit-cloth, and cushion, "that all things may be done orderly and decently in the church."

In the next century, there is a record of an order sent to England for gold-leaf to enrich a chancel, which was to be made gorgeous with an original painting of an angel holding back a crimson curtain, draped with a golden cord and tassel.

The pulpits in the old churches were placed at an angle, if the church were in the form of a cross; or if the building were an oblong on one side. These pulpits were so high that, unless the preacher were very tall, nothing could be seen by the congregation but the top of his head. Bishop Meade confesses that when he was to speak from one of these old box-pulpits, he would often hurry to church before his hearers, in order

Ye Pulpit.

to pile up bricks or boards on which to stand. The good bishop must sometimes have found his thoughts sadly distracted from the sermon by the necessity of keeping his balance on his improvised platform.

The sharp distinction of classes, which was so marked a feature of the Cavalier Colonies, showed itself even in church. Certain pews were set apart and marked "Magistrates" and "Magistrates' Ladies." Into these the great folks marched solemnly on Sundays, followed by their slaves bearing prayer-books, and never suspecting that their conduct was at variance with gospel principles. The great families kept their private pews for generations, and held firmly to their privileges. Matthew Kemp, as churchwarden, was commended by his vestry for displacing "a presuming woman, who would fain have taken a pew above her degree." In the very earliest church, Lord De la Warre's seat was upholstered in green velvet with a green "cooshoon;" Governor Spotswood's pew in Bruton Parish Church at Williamsburg was raised from the floor, and covered with a canopy, while the interior was ornamented with his name in gilt letters. In 1750, it was ordered by the vestry of St. Paul's Church, Norfolk, that "three captains and Mr. Charles Sweeny be allowed to build a gallery reaching from the gallery of Mr.

John Taylor to the school-boys' gallery, to be theirs and their heirs' forever."

Washington's pew was an ample square, fitted with cushions for sitting and kneeling. The Puritans would have thought it a glaring iniquity to pay such heed to creature comfort in the house of God. They would have been more in sympathy with the Virginia dame of high degree who, in tardy atonement for her pride, directed that her body be buried under the pavement in the aisle occupied by the poor of the church, that they might trample on her dust. Such gloomy and ascetic associations with the house of God were rare at the South. The church was a centre of cheerfulness, and the Sabbath was supposed to be a day of innocent enjoyment. All work was frowned upon as inconsistent with a due observance of its sanctity, however; and the Grand Jury in Middlesex County, Virginia, in 1704, presented Thomas Simms, for travelling on the road on Sunday with a loaded beast, William Montague and Garrett Minor for bringing oysters ashore on the Sabbath, James Senis for swearing and cursing on the holy day; but outside such restrictions as these, no Blue Laws enforced gloom as part of the decorum of Sunday-keeping.

When the church-bell, hung usually from the

bough of a tree, began to ring for service, the roads were filled with worshippers moving church-ward, full of peace and good-will. First might be seen the young men on horseback, with the tails of their coats carefully pinned in front, to protect them from the sweat of their horses' flanks. Lumbering slowly after these equestrians came the great family-coaches, from which the ladies are assisted by the dismounted gallants. Every young damsel is planning some social festivity. Before or after service, invitations are given, and visits of weeks in length are arranged at the church door. It is to be feared that these colonial maidens sometimes allow their thoughts to wander in sermon-time, from their quaint little prayer-books, with their uneven type and crooked f's, and that they are thinking of dinners while they confess themselves sinners. But their levity is not treated severely by the priest, for he is as eager for his Madeira as his young parishioners are eager for their minuet.

They were jolly dogs, those colonial clergymen of the Church of England in the eighteenth century, and no more to be taken seriously than Friar Tuck, whose apostolic successors they were. Parishioners who wished spiritual counsel had difficulty in finding the parson. In the morning he was fox-hunting, in the afternoon he was over (or under) the dining-table, and the midnight candle shone on his wine-cup and dice-box.

Like their brethren across the Altantic, the colonial clergy were strong on doctrine. "They abhorred popery, atheism, and idolatries in general, and hiccupped 'Church and State!' with fervor." Yet their morals were at so low an ebb as to justify the complaint made against them that they were "such as wore black coats and could gabble in a pulpit, roar in a tavern, exact from their parishioners, and rather by their dissoluteness destroy than feed their flock."

One clergyman assaulted a dignitary in vestry-meeting, pulling off his wig and subjecting him to various indignities, and capped the climax of audacity by preaching the next Sunday from the text: "I contended with them and cursed them, and smote certain of them and pulled off their hair." Another minister fought a duel behind his church, and a third, the Rev. Thomas Blewer (pronounced probably *Blower*), was presented by the Grand Jury as a common swearer. All efforts to reform the clergy were in vain. Ministers were sometimes tried for drunkenness, and some of the tests of what constitutes drunkenness were laid down by the court: "Sitting an hour or longer in the company where they are drinking strong drink and in the mean time drinking of healths, or otherwise taking the cups as they come round, like the rest of the company; striking or challenging or threatening to fight." Staggering, reeling, and incoherent speech are justly regarded as suspicious circumstances, and the advice continues: "Let the proof of these signs proceed so far till the judges conclude that behavior at such time was scandalous, undecent, unbecoming the dignity of a minister." There is unfortunately only too clear a case against the colonial clergy; but it is only fair to take into account the condition of the church at home. If the clergymen in Maryland and Virginia gambled and drank, so did those in England and Wales. Did not Sterne grace the cassock? Did not Gay propose taking orders for a living, and did not Swift write from a deanery stuff too vile for print? There was some talk at one time of sending this great Dr. Swift over to Virginia as a bishop, and a worthy one he would have been, to such a church.

The eighteenth century was a period of decadence in the colonial ministry. Things had not always been so bad. When the first settlers came to America, the clergymen who accompanied them were men of sterling worth and character. They were moved by a hope of converting the Indians, and came in a true missionary spirit. The journals of those adventurers testify to the courage with which their chaplain braved dangers and bore discomforts. "By unprosperous winds," they say, "we were kept six weeks in sight of England; all which time Master Hunt, our preacher, was so weake and sicke that few expected his recovery. Yet, although we were but twentie myles from his habitation, and notwithstanding the stormy weather, nor the scandalous imputations against him, all this could never force from him so much as a seeming desire to leave the businesse." All through the journey he was brave and cheerful, though there was a constant ferment of wrath in that hot-headed ship's company, which might have ended in bloodshed, "had he not, with the water of patience and his godly exhortations, but chiefly by his true, devoted example, quenched those flames of envy and detraction." Finally, after the fire at Jamestown, Master Hunt lost all his library and "all he had but the cloathes on his backe, yet none never heard him repine at his loss."

Following Hunt came the good Whitaker, "a schollar, a graduate, a preacher well born and well friended in England," who from conscientious desire to help the savages left "his warm nest and, to the wonder of his kinsmen, and to the amazement of them that knew him," undertook this perilous enterprise. Of such pith and worth were these first priests; but the Indian massacre made a great change. Friendly intercourse with the natives being cut off, there was no chance for missionary work among them, and the plantations were too far apart to make a vigorous church life possible. The pay was small and the field barren, so that there was little temptation either to the ambitious and intellectual, or to the spiritually minded class of the clergy, to come to America. They were as a rule, therefore, the ignorant, the dissipated, and the *mauvais sujets* who filled the colonial livings. Yet at the lowest ebb there were exceptions to this rule. There, for instance, was Rector Robert Rose, whose tombstone describes him as discharging with the most tender piety the " domestick " duties of husband, father, son, and brother, and in short as " a friend to the whole human race." His journal gives a glimpse of his relations with his parish, very cheering in the dreary waste of quarrels and bickering so common in those days. On one occasion, during a drouth, when a famine threatened, he told his people that corn could be had from him. On the appointed day a crowd gathered before his house. He asked the applicants if they had brought money to pay for the corn. Some answered cheerfully, " Yes," others murmured disconsolately, " No." The good priest then said: " You who have money can get your corn anywhere, but these poor fellows with no money shall have my corn."

He was quite human, this old parson, and liked his glass of "Fyal" or Madeira, but he knew when to stop, and he feared not to rebuke the rich and great among his parishioners when he saw them making too merry. He enters in his journal the date of a call on one of his leading families, when he found the father absent at a cock-fight. The rector adds the significant memorandum: "Suffer it no more!"

In spite of a few bright exceptions like this, it is idle to deny that the relations between parish and clergy in the Southern church ill bore comparison with those of the Puritan and his minister; and this not because of doctrine, but chiefly because the Puritan minister represented the free choice of the people, who supported him willingly, and looked upon him with reverence, as the messenger of the Lord. In South Carolina, where the clergy were chosen by the vestries, the same harmony and good-will existed, but the church in Virginia writhed under the injustice of taxation without representation.

The parishioners were expected to receive and maintain the clergyman appointed them without criticism or question. How any attempt on the part of these vestries to discipline or dismiss the minister they supported was received, we may judge from this letter, sent by Governor Spotswood to the churchwardens and vestry of South Farnham parish in 1716:

"Gentlemen: I'm not a little surprised at the sight of an order of yours, wherein you take upon you to suspend from his office a clergyman who for near sixteen years has served as your minister. . . . As no vestry in England has ever pretended to set themselves up as judges over their ministers, so I know no law of this country that has given such authority to the vestry here. If a clergyman transgresses against the canons of the church, he is to be tried before a proper judicature, and though in this country there be no bishops to apply to, yet there is a substitute for a bishop in your diocesan. . . . In case of the misbehavior of your clergyman, you may be his accusers, but in no case his judges; but much less are you empowered to turn him out without showing cause."

This haughty language recalls the messages of Charles the First to his parliament. Yet in spite of his support of the priest against the parish, the Governor never dreamed of recognizing him as his own equal. Some years later, when the stately old aristocrat was in his grave, a member of the clergy sued for the hand of his widow, Lady Spotswood. The reverend suitor writes after a very humble and apologetic fashion: "Madam," he begins, "by diligently perusing your letter I perceive there is a material argument—upon which your strongest objection against completing my happiness would seem to depend, viz.: That you would incur ye censure of ye world for marrying a person in ye station of my station and character. By which I understand that you think it a diminution of your honour and ye dignity of your family to marry a person in ye station of a clergyman. Now, if I can make it appear that ye ministerial office is an employment in its nature ye most honorable and in its effects ye most beneficial to mankind, I hope your objections will immediately vanish—that you will keep me no longer in suspense and misery, but consummate my happiness." After a long enumeration of the dignities, spiritual rather than social, appertaining to the clergy, he closes thus: "And, therefore, if a gentleman of this sacred and honourable character should be married to a lady, though of ye greatest extraction and most excellent personal qualities (which I am sensible you are endowed with), it can be no disgrace to her or her family; nor draw the censures of ye world upon them for such an action." Such language is in curious contrast with the attitude of New England, where the praise bestowed on a woman by Cotton Mather as the highest possible compliment was, that she was worthy to be the wife of a priest.

The chief cause of irritation between parson and parish in the colonial church was from the beginning the question of the ministers' salaries. In some places these were very small. It appears, for instance, in the record book of the church at Edenton, in North Carolina, that Parson Garzia in the year 1736, was paid only £5 for holding divine service. But in Maryland and Virginia the salaries were frequently higher than those paid in New England. In each Virginia borough a hundred acres were set off as a glebe, or parsonage farm. Besides this and the salary, there were fees of twenty shillings for a wedding by license and five shillings for every wedding by banns, beside forty shillings for a funeral sermon. It is easier to understand the fulsomeness of these old funeral discourses when we learn how well they were paid for, and realize that, in common honesty, the minister was bound to render a forty-shilling certificate of character to the deceased.

As time went on, the salary question became a burning issue. The plantations being so widely separated, quarrels often arose as to the portion of the parish on which the chief burden of the minister's support should fall. In the records of the very early Virginia church history, we come upon an instance of this in the proceedings in Lower Norfolk County, at a court held 25th May, 1640.

"Whereas the inhabitants of this parrishe beinge this day conevented for the providinge of themselves an able minister to instruct them concerning their soules' health, mr. Thomas Harrison tharto hath tendered his service to god and the said inhabitants in that behalf wch his said tender is well liked of, with the genall approbacon of the said Inhabitants, the parishoners of the parishe church at mr. Sewell's Point who to testifie their zeale and willingness to p'mote gods service doe hereby p'mise (and the court now sittinge doth likewise order and establish the same) to pay one hundreth pounds starling yearely to the sd mr. Harrison, soe Longe as hee shall continue a minister to the said Parishe in recompence of his paynes."

This arrangement apparently did not long prove satisfactory, for the record goes on to state that

"Whereas there is a difference amongst the Inhabitants of the fforesaid Pishe, concerninge the imployinge of a minister beinge now entertayned to live amongst them, The Inhabitants from Danyell Tanner's Creek and upward the three branches of Elizabeth river (in respect they are the greatest number of tithable persons) not thinknge it fitt nor equall that they shall pay the greatest pte of one hundred pownds w^h is by the ffore sd order allotted for the ministers annuall stipend, unlesse the sd minister may teach and Instruct them as often as he shall teach at ye Pishe church siytuate at mr. Sewell's Pointe. It is therefore agreed amongst the sd Inhabitants that the sd minister shall teach evie other Sunday amongst the Inhabitants of Elizabeth River at the house of Robert Glasscocke untill a convenyent church be built and Erected there for gods service w^h is agreed to bee finished at the charge of the Inhabitants of Elizabeth River before the first day of May next ensueinge."

However little value they might set on Gospel privileges, these Danyell Tanner's Creek men meant to have what they paid for, or cease their payments.

A Virginia statue of 1696 declared that each minister of a parish should receive an annual stipend of sixteen thousand pounds of tobacco. This amounted to about £140, as tobacco sold for many years at two-pence the pound. But, in the year 1755, there was a shortage in the tobacco crop, and the legislature passed an act enabling the inhabitants of the county to discharge their tobacco-debts in money for the present year. The clergy seem to have made no active opposition; but five years later, when a similar law was passed, and tobacco rose sharply in price, they took alarm, and started a violent campaign in defence of their rights. The Reverend John Camm published a sarcastic pamphlet on "The Two Penny Act." This was answered by Colonel Bland and Colonel Carter in two very plain-spoken documents. Camm again rode a tilt against them in a pamphlet called "The Colonels Dismounted."

The community began by laughing, but ended by getting angry. Mr. Camm could find no more printers in Virginia, and was obliged to go to Maryland to carry on the war. The contest grew to larger proportions. It crossed the ocean and was laid before the king, who, always glad of an opportunity to repress anything which looked like popular sovereignty, declared in favor of the clergy. Armed thus by royal approbation, the parsons brought their case to trial. The Rev. James Maury brought suit in Hanover County against the collector. The defendants pleaded the law of 1758, but the plaintiff demurred on the ground that that law, never having been confirmed by the king, was null and void. The case was tried, Mr. Lyons arguing for the plaintiff and Mr. Lewis for the defendant. The court sustained the demurrer, and the clergy looked upon their case as won. Lewis was so sure of it that he retired from the cause, telling his clients that there was nothing more to be done in the matter. Nothing remained but for a jury to fix the amount of damages.

In this desperate state of affairs, Patrick Henry, though almost unknown at the bar, was called in, and he agreed to argue the case at the next term. On the first of December, accordingly, he came into the court-room, to find it densely packed with an excited throng of listeners. The bench was filled with clergymen. In the magistrate's seat sat the young orator's own father. The occasion might well have tried the nerve of an older and more experienced speaker. Lyons opened the cause for the clergy, with the easy assurance of one who sees his case already won. He told the jury that the law of 1758 had been set aside, and that it only remained for them to enforce the law of 1748 by awarding suitable damages to his clients, whom he exalted to the skies in a eulogy which might have better fitted better men. Lyons sat down, and young Henry rose. Awkwardly and falteringly he began, in painful contrast to the easy address of Lyons. The plaintiffs on the bench looked at each other with smiles of derision. The people, who realized that his cause was theirs, hung their heads; but only for a moment. The young orator, whose timid commencement had caused winks and nods of satisfaction to pass along the bench of the clergy, suddenly changed his whole attitude. All at once he shook off embarrassment, and roused himself like a lion brought to bay. The people at first were cheered, then became intoxicated with his eloquence. The clergy listened to the flood of sarcasm and invective till they could bear no more, and fled from the bench as from a pillory. Henry's eloquence swept the jury, who returned at once with a verdict of *one penny damages* for the clergy. The people, wild with delight, seized their hero and carried him out on their shoulders. Henceforward he was a marked man, and for years, Wirt tells us, when the old people wished to praise any one's eloquence, they would say: "He is almost equal to Patrick when he pled against the parsons."

With so much hostile feeling toward their clergy, how shall we account for the strong affection felt by the Virginians for their church? I find the explanation in that loyalty to lost causes and that aristocratic conservatism which always marked the Cavalier. These, in spite of the debasement of the clergy, the zeal of the "New Lights," the allurements of Rome, and the eloquence of Whitefield, Fox, and the Wesleys, long kept the Cavalier Colonies true to the church of their fathers. It was not till the church allied itself with the king against the people in the Revolutionary struggle, that its doom fell.

It was a matter of course that self-interest as well as sentiment should lead the clergy to espouse the cause of England. In a letter, dated 1766, the Rev. John Camm writes from Virginia to a Mrs. McClurg in the mother-country. He begins, as is natural, with what is nearest his heart, namely his own affairs, and requests the lady to use her influence with Mr. Pitt to secure him a Living of one hundred pounds a year. Fearing that his request is too modest: "Observe," he says, "tho' a Living of one hundred nett will *do*, I care not how much larger the Living shall be. If by conversing with the Great, you have learnt their manners, and are unwilling to bestow so considerable a favour on a friend without some way or other finding your account in the transaction, which the unpolished call a bribe, you shall make your own terms with me. I will submit to what you think reasonable, and then, you know, the larger the Living or Post is, the better for both."

This pious worthy, having thus disposed of the affairs of the church, next deals in the same public spirited manner with the affairs of the colonial politics:

"One of our most active, flaming and applauded sons of liberty, Col. Rich'd Henry Lee, who burnt poor Mercer in effigy, raised a mob on Archy Ritchie, etc., etc., etc., has been lately blown up in the Publick Prints, it is said, by Mr. James Mercer. It appears that Lee, previous to his Patriotism, had made interest to be made Stamp Master himself, from letters it seems now in the possession of Col. Mercer, so that Lee will find it difficult hereafter to deceive anybody into an opinion of his Patriotism."

Posterity has quite definitely settled the question of the comparative patriotism of Col. Lee and the Rev. John Camm, and only wonders that a shrewd people tolerated that ecclestiastical fraud so long. Peace to his ashes! since he and his fellows have given way to good and sincere men who have purged the church of her disgrace and brought her back to her older and better traditions.

A gentleman of the old school, in cocked hat and knee-breeches, once said to Madison that a man might be a *Christian* in any church, but a *gentleman* must belong to the Church of England.

His Education

His Education

GOVERNOR BERKELEY, that old stumbling-block-head who stopped the wheels of progress in Virginia for fifty years, wrote to the English Commissioners in 1670: "I thank God there are no free schools nor printing; and I hope we shall not have, for learning hath brought disobedience and heresy and sects into the world, and printing hath divulged them, and libels against the best government. God keep us from both!"

The bigoted Sir William set forth but too accurately the condition of affairs not only in Virignia, but in Maryland as well. It is impossible to avoid noting the striking contrast between the South and New England, where, by this time, every colony except Rhode Island had made education compulsory, where the school-house and the church stood side by side in every village. An old New England statute commands that "every township, after the

Lord hath increased them to the number of fifty households, shall appoint one to teach all the children to write and read, and when any town shall increase to the number of a hundred families, they shall set up a grammar school." All the energy of the Puritan which was not absorbed in religion vented itself on education. Ambition turned its current to learning as more desirable than wealth. "Child," said a New England matron to her boy, "if God make thee a good Christian and a good scholar, thou hast all that thy mother ever asked for thee."

Such a spirit bred a race of readers and students, trained to sift arguments and to weigh reasons. No such devotion to books or scholarship prevailed at the South. Yet when the Revolution came, the most thrilling eloquence, the highest statesmanship, the greatest military genius were found among these Southerners. Their education had been different from that of the Puritans, but it had been an education none the less. The Cavalier had been trained in the school of politics, in the responsibilities of power, and in the traditions of greatness.

The very absence of the reading habit tended to develop action, and the power of thinking out problems afresh, unhampered by the trammels of other men's thoughts. The haughtiness begotten by slave-holding made it doubly hard for the master to bow the knee even to a sovereign. The habit of command and responsibility of power, which shone on the battlefield and in the council-chamber, were learned on the lonely estates, where each planter was a king. Behind all these elements of training were the ideals which moulded the mind and the character.

Berkeley's taunting question to Bacon, "Have you forgot to be *a gentleman?*" owed its sting to this suggestion that he had been false to the traditions of his class. If we hold that tact and courtesy and gracious hospitality are results of education, we must admit that the Puritans of New England might have learned much from their neighbors in Maryland and Virginia. The education of politics, of power, of high traditions in virtue and in manners the Colonial Cavalier possessed. The education of books he lacked. Here and there, however, we find traces of some omnivorous reader even in the earliest times. Books were highly valued and treasured by generation after generation. We find among the old wills that "Richard Russell left Richard Yates 'a booke called Lyons play,' 'John porter junr. six books' 'John porter (1) my exec'r, ten books,' 'Katherin Greene three bookes,' 'One book to Sarah Dyer,' 'unto Wm. Greene his wife two books & her mother a booke,' 'Anna

Godby two books,' 'Jno. Abell One booke in Quarto,' 'Richard Lawrence One booke.'*

---

*V. *Library* of Edmund Berkeley, Esq., Member of the Council (Died 15 Dec. 1718), from an inventory taken the 18 and 19 days of June, 1719:

The whole Duty of Mann One old Bible and one old comon pray^r book The Christian Sacrifice The great Duty of frequenting the Christian Sacrifice A Brief chronicle of the Civil Wars of England and Ireland. Cavalrie the first Book The common prayer book the best companion. Janna Divoram. Contemplations on the State of Mann the first part of the English Dixtionary The Wel Spring of Sciences The Young Clerk guide A compendium of physick The Athenian Oracle A Guide to Constables Some consideration touching the Stile of the Holy Scriptures. A perfect Guide for a Studious Young Lawyer The p^{r}sent State of London. a Profitable book for those that are burnt with Gunpowder. The first part of the English Dictionary a Compleat history of England The lives of the noble Grecians and Romans. The Tragedy of Darius and Julius Cæsar A Compleat Collections of all the Laws of Virginia The new world of English words. The history of the Jews. The Countrey Justice The first part of Compleat Histrey The Expotion of the Creed The Surgeons mate An Essay concerning human understanding a Breife Treatise of Testaments The Decameron A Compendius Dictionary Lexicon Manuale. Lord Delamers Works. Sixteen sermons on several occasions ffarquhars Works. An abridgment of all the Statutes in fforce The standard of the Quakers. The Hearts Ease. A Tryal of Faith Several Discourses of the great Duties of Natural Religion The Works of Josephus in three Volumes Doctor Reads Works. Abridgment of the Statutes of King Wm. Plutarchs Morals. Bethel or a fform for ffamilys

THE COLONIAL CAVALIER.

Master Ralph Wormeley's library numbered several hundred volumes, and a man might have

Discourses on the History of the whole world of wisdom the second and third books. Mr. John Banisters Works. The History of ffrance the first and fourth volumes of the turkish spy Sermons on several occasions resolutions and devisions of Cases of Conscience Plutarchs Morals the Second Volume and the third. A Manual Anatomy England's General Description Shakespears Works. Second Volume of Tom Browns Works Copies of Certain Letters. Ancient and the present State of the Empire of Germany. The Shepards oracles. Physoignomie and Chiromancy The Genral View of the Holy Scriptures The practice of piety The great law of consideration Trigonometrie Of generosity and constancy in the faith The History of the Revolutions in Sweeden The Marrow of Chyrurgery Toleration discuss'd. Letters of Remarkables in Switzerland The office of Executors a Companion for a Chyrurgeon The Critick The Lively Oracles The heaven of health The history of the Conquest of China Valentine and Orson. a Discourse on the Sacraments Some Motives to the Love of God. an Introduction to the Skill of Musick. Sermons and Discourses some of which never before printed. The Nature of Truth discuss'd The Method of physick The new London Dispensatory. a Compendius Dictionary Milk for Babes an Introduction to the Eight parts of Latin speech The use of piety The European Mercury The Books of psalms. Notes on Mr. Lockes Essay of Human Understanding Britains Remembrancer An Infallible way to Contentment a view of all the religions in the world A Description of the Little world. The portraiture of his sacred Maj^{ty} in his solitudes and suferings The London Dispensatory English Examples a Short Introduction to Gramar a Short Catechisme The Esopps ffables Works of Mr Thos Southerne Eight Lattin Books.

found enough among them to gratify any inclination. If his tastes were frivolous, here were "fifty comodys and tragedies," and "The Genteel Siner." Were he an epicure, he might regale himself with "the body of cookery," and revel in its appetizing recipes for potpies and the proper method of roasting a sucking pig; and if his mind were piously inclined, the resources of the library were unlimited. Side by side on its shelves stood "No Cross, No Crowne," "The ffamous Doct^r Usher's Body of Divinity," Doct^r ffuller's Holy State," and last and longest, the ninety-six sermons of the good parson Andros.

Some of these old colonial sermons came to an unprofitable end. A bundle of them was laid away in a drawer, and, when sought for, it was learned that they had been torn up and used by the damsels of the household as curling-papers. The writer might have been at least half-satisfied in the reflection that his discourses had touched the head, if not the heart.

In spite of all the old inventories which are being brought to light to show the existence of books and book lovers in the South, the fact remains that the Cavalier was no bookworm. He felt that a boy who had learned to ride, to shoot, and to speak the truth, had received the rudiments at least of education. Whatever he learned more than this was acquired either in the old *field-school* or more often from a private tutor, usually a clergyman of the Church of England. Some attempts were made by private persons to found public-schools. In 1634, Benjamin Sym devised two hundred acres of land on the Pocosan River, together with the milk and increase of eight cows, for " the maintenance of a learned, honest man, to keep, upon the said ground, a Free-School for the education of the children of Elizabeth City and Kiquotan, from Mary's Mount downward to the Pocosan River."

" Richard Russell in his will made July 24th, 1667, and proved December 16th, the same year, now among the records of Lower Norfolk county, declared: 'the other pte of my Estate I give & bequeath One pte of itt unto Six of the poorest mens Children in Eliz: Riv'r, to pay for their Teaching to read & after these six are entred then if Six more comes I give a pte allsoe to Enter them in like manner.' "

In spite of private gifts, and individual effort, and public Acts of Assembly, the school system of New England did not and could not thrive at the South, because it was out of harmony with the spirit and institutions of the people. The plantations were so separated that any assembling of the children was difficult, the spirit of caste was too strong to encourage the free mingling of rich and poor, and the traditions of the Cavalier were not traditions of scholarship. The sword, not the pen, had always been the weapon of the gentleman. Montrose, and not Milton, was his hero. When Captain Smith proudly boasted that he did not sit mewed up in a library writing of other men's exploits, but that what his sword did, his pen writ, he expressed the ideal of the Colonial Cavalier.

"I observe," quoth Spotswood ironically to the Virginia Burgesses, "that the grand ruling party in your House has not furnished chairmen of two of your standing committees who can spell English or write common-sense, as the grievances under their own hand-writing will manifest."

Ebenezer Cook in his "Voyage to Maryland," writes with acrimonious sarcasm of "A reverend judge who, to the shame of all the Bench, could write his name." The jest of the Sot-Weed Factor scarcely outstripped the sober truth, and a century later the general ignorance was almost as dense. Several instances are on record where the servant signed his name and the master made his mark. The cross or other conventional sign was not uncommon, and in general the letters of the names are evolved slowly and painfully, as by men more apt with the gun than with the quill.

Hugh Jones, a Fellow of William and Mary College, writes of his countrymen that, for the most part, they are only desirous of learning what is absolutely necessary, in the shortest way. To meet this peculiarity Mr. Jones states that he has designed a royal road to learning, consisting of a series of text-books embracing an *Accidence to Christianity*, an *Accidence to the Mathematicks*, and an *Accidence to the English Tongue*. This last is "for the use of such boys and men as have never learned Latin, and for the Benefit of the Female Sex."

The Bishop of London addressed a circular to the Virginia clergy inquiring as to the condition of their parishes. To the question, "Are there any schools in your parish?" the almost invariable answer was: "None." To the question, "Is there any parish library?" but a single affirmative response was received. One minister replied, "We have the *The Book of Homilies*, *The Whole Duty of Man*, and *The Singing Psalms*."

It may be to this very scarcity of books that we owe that originality and vigor of thought which distinguished the leaders of the Revolution. Governor Page reported Patrick Henry as saying to him, "Naiteral parts is better than all the larnin upon yearth," and when to *naiteral parts* we add the mastery of a few English classics, we touch the secret of the dignity and virility which mark the utterances of these men who had known so little school-training.

THE COLONIAL CAVALIER.

Randolph of Roanoke, the youngest son of his widowed mother, was taught by her as a little child. As he grew older he was left a good deal to his own devices, but his mind was not idle, and he had access to an unusually good library. Before he was ten, he had read Voltaire's "History of Charles XII.," "Reynard the Fox," and odd volumes of *The Spectator*. The "Arabian Nights" and Shakespeare were his delight. "I had read them," he writes, "with Don Quixote, Quintus Curtius, Plutarch, Pope's Homer, Robinson Crusoe, Gulliver, Tom Jones, Orlando Furioso, and Thomson's Seasons, before I was eleven years old."

Washington, unlike most of his compeers, was sent to school, first in the little cabin taught by the sexton of the church, a man named Hobby, and afterward to a more advanced school taught by a Mr. Williams. Here he decorated his writing and ciphering books, school-boy fashion, with nondescript birds done in pen-flourishes, and with amateur profile portraits. Here also he copied legal forms, bills of exchange, bonds, etc., till he acquired that methodical habit which afterward stood him in good stead. There were good and faithful teachers in those days, though they were not too common. The Scotch seem to have done most of the teaching in the colonies, and to have done it well. Jefferson recalls the "mouldy pies and good teaching" of the Scotch minister who taught him the languages; and many a Scotch name figures in the list of parish school-teachers.

In an old file of the *Maryland Gazette* we may read the advertisement of John and Sally Stott, who propose to open a school "where English, arithmetic, book-keeping, mensuration, knitting, sewing and sample-work on cat-gut and muslin are to be taught in an easy and intelligible manner."

The charges for schooling were not extravagant. The Reverend Devereux Jarratt taught a "plain school" for the equivalent of about thirty-three dollars a year. A tutor from London received a salary of thirty pounds sterling, and Jonathan Boucher charged for tuition twenty-five pounds a year, "the boy to bring his own bed."

Boucher was at one time tutor to Parke Custis, then a somewhat headstrong boy of sixteen. Young Custis wished to travel abroad with his tutor, but Washington wrote to Mr. Boucher: "I can not help giving it as my opinion that his education is by no means ripe enough for a travelling tour. Not that I think his becoming a mere scholar is a desirable education for a gentleman, but I conceive a knowledge of books is the basis upon which all other knowledge is to be built, and in travelling he is to become acquainted with men and things rather than books." Later in the letter he adds: "It is to be expected that every man who travels with a view of observing the laws and customs of other countries should be able to give some description of the situation and government of his own."

Boucher took just the opposite ground from his patron. He argued that the best education consisted in mingling with men and seeing the culture of other lands. He lamented the provinciality of Virginia and its lack of intercourse with the great world. "Saving here and there a needy emigrant from Great Britain, an illiterate captain of a ship, or a subaltern merchant, to whom," he asks, "can a Virginia youth apply for a specimen of the manners, etc., of any other people?"

The majority of the landed gentry were in sympathy with the views of Boucher rather than with those of Washington. Travel and education abroad, especially in England, were universally desired, and the influence on the colonies was marked, as the lad brought back with him from Oxford the views of the Cavaliers and their descendants, as the ship which bore him brought back the carved furniture, the massive plate, the leather-bound books, the coat of arms, and the panels for the hall fireplace.

The record of matriculations at Oxford contains

many colonial names. Here is "Henry Fitzhugh, s. William, of Virginia, Gent." (Christ Church) matriculated at the age of fifteen. Christopher and Peter Robinson, and Robert Yates, set down as from "*Insula Virginiæ*," register at Oriel, and Lewis Burwell at Balliol. The average age of matriculation among these colonial youth is eighteen; but boys were often sent to England, or "home," as the colonists delighted to call it, long before they were old enough for University life.

Governor Spotswood's grandsons were sent over seas to Eton by their guardian, Colonel Moore, their father being dead. They boarded with a Mrs. Young, who showed a wonderfully good and tender heart, for when their guardian ceased to send remittances and the poor boys were left without resources, this kind landlady not only remitted the price of their board, which with charges for candles, fire and mending amounted to over twenty-eight pounds sterling, but actually supplied them with pocket-money to the extent of three pounds, and paid the expenses of "salt money, cost of montem poles, and montem dinner." When they left, Alexander wrote from London to their benefactress a manly if somewhat prim little letter, commencing: "Hon[d] Madam, I write by this opportunity to thank you for all your past favors to me and my brother. I hope it will be in my power one day or another to make you amends for all you have done for us," and signing himself, "Your humble servant, Alexander Spotswood." It is gratifying to know that these protestations did not come to naught, but that the good lady was repaid, not only in money, but in the life-long gratitude of the boys, who became distinguished American citizens.

The inheritance of a high and quick spirit came fairly to the boys of their race. Some quarter of a century before this letter was written, the Virginia *Gazette* printed a communication from the father of these lads, then himself a boy. It is headed "An Hint for a Hint," and runs:

"Mr. Parks,

"I have learnt my Book, so far as to be able to read plain English, when printed in your Papers, and finding in one of them my Papa's name often mentioned by a scolding man called Edwin Conway, I asked my Papa whether he did not design to answer him. But he replyd: 'No child, this is a better Contest for you that are a school Boy, for it will not become me to answer every Fool in his Folly, as the Lesson you learned the other day of the Lion and the Ass may teach you.' This Hint being given me, I copied out the said

Lesson and now send you the same for my Answer to Mr. Conway's Hint from

"Sir, your Humble Servant

"JOHN SPOTSWOOD.

"Fab. 10. A Lion and an Ass.

"An Ass was so hardy once as to fall a Mopping and Braying at a Lion. The Lion began at first to shew his Teeth and to stomach the Affront, But upon second Thoughts, Well, says he, Jeer on and be an Ass still, take notice only by the way, that it is the Baseness of your Character that has saved your Carcass."

No doubt young John and Alexander treasured this piece of youthful audacity as a precious tradition to be told and retold to admiring schoolmates at Montem dinner, under the shadow of Eton Towers.

In the Bland letters, there is an itemized account of the charges for a colonial boy at boarding school. Master Bland's expenses, when under the tuition of Mr. Clark, amounted to twenty-four pounds, ten shillings and two pence, and include the bills sent in by the apothecary, hosier, linen-draper, music-master and "taylor," and also the charges for "weekly allowance and lent, shugar and blackshoe."

The charge for *shugar* is twelve shillings and

ninepence, which seems exorbitant in our day of cheap sweets. Master Bland's second half-year's account charges for "milliner, board, coal and candles, pocket-money and stockener."

There is no record of the profit Master Bland received from his schooling abroad, but it is to be feared that he shared the character of his young fellow-countrymen, of whom Jones reports that "they are noted to be more apt to spoil their school-fellows than improve themselves." The wildness of the young colonial students this reverend apologist accounts for very ingeniously, by explaining that the trouble lies in their being "put to learn to persons that know little of their temper, who keep them drudging in pedantick methods, too tedious for their volatile genius."

The young Colonial Cavaliers exercised their *volatile genius* at home as well as abroad, as any one may know who turns the yellow pages of the manuscript college records at William and Mary. Under Stith's presidency we find "Y^e following orders unanimously agreed to":

"1. Ordered y^t no scholar belonging to any school in the college, of what age, rank or quality so ever, do keep any race horse at ye college in ye town, or anywhere in the neighborhood, y^t they be not anyway concerned in making races or in backing or abetting those made by others, and y^t

all race-horses kept in ye neighborhood of ye college and belonging to any of ye scholars, be immediately dispatched and sent off and never again brought back, and all this under pain of ye severest animadversion and punishment."

A second ordinance forbids any scholar belonging to the college, "to appear playing or betting at ye billiard or other gaming tables, or to be any way concerned in keeping or fighting cocks, under pain of ye like severe animadversions or punishments."

They were an unruly and turbulent set of school-boys, these collegians, and the college records are full of their misdoings. Thomas Byrd, being brought before the Faculty on a charge of breaking windows "in a rude and riotous mannor," was sentenced to submit to a whipping in the Grammar-School, or be expelled the college. The blood of the Byrds rebelled against such ignominy, and the boy refused to submit. His father then appeared before the Faculty and offered to compel him to obey, but this vicarious submission was considered inadequate, and he was dropped from the college. Again, it appears, that "whereas John Hyde Saunders has lately behaved himself in a very impudent and unheard-of mannor to the master of the Grammar-School," he is directed to quit the college. The ushers are ordered to visit the rooms of the young gentlemen at least three times a week, after nine o'clock at night, and report to the president any irregularities.

"No boy to presume to go into the kitchen." "No victuals sent to private rooms." "No boy to lounge upon the college steps." So run the rules. They further provide "y^t a person be appointed to hear such boys as shall be recommended by their parents or guardians, a chapter in the Bible every school-day at 12 o'clock, and y^t he have ye yearly salary of one pistole for each boy so recommended." All these regulations, "animadversions," and punishments make us realize that in spite of its high-sounding charter, William and Mary was, after all, only a big boarding-school.

When its charter was granted, a curious condition was attached, providing that the president and professors should yearly offer two copies of Latin verses to the Governor or Lieutenant-Governor of Virginia. The bargain seems to have been strictly kept, for *The Gazette* records:

"On this day sen-night, the president, masters and scholars of William and Mary College went, according to their annual custom, in a body to the Governor's, to present His Honor with two copies of Latin verses in obedience to their charter, as a grateful acknowledgement for two valuable tracts of land given the said college by their late Majesties, King William and Queen Mary. Mr President delivered the verses to His Honor and two of the young gentlemen spoke them."

In 1700, the college authorities ushered in the century with a grand celebration, including prize declamations and various exercises. The novel and exciting entertainment roused such an interest that visitors came from Annapolis and the Maryland shore, and even from the far-away colony of New York, while Indians thronged the streets to watch the gayety. The town then was at the height of its prosperity.

Not content with a palace, a capitol, and a college, Williamsburg actually aspired to own a bookstore, which was after all not altogether unreasonable, since there was no considerable one south of Boston. Accordingly the college authorities met to consider the matter, and finally resolved that—

"Mr Wm Parks intending to open a book-seller's shop in this Town, and having proposed to furnish the students of this College with such books at a reasonable price as the Masters shall direct him to send for, and likewise to take all the school-books now in the College and pay 35 p. cent on the sterling cost to make it currency, his proposals are unanimously agreed to."

The first building of William and Mary College

was planned, so they say, by Sir Christopher Wren, but it was burned down, one night only five years after the grand celebration, "the governor and all the gentlemen in town coming to the lamentable spectacle; many of them getting out of their beds." Again and again the building has suffered from the flames. Yet as it stands there to-day— with its stiff, straight walls stained and weather-beaten, its bricks laid up in the good old English fashion of stretchers and headers, its steps worn with the tread of generations—it is full of a pensive charm. Its record is one for Virginians to be proud of, since as one of them boasts:

"It has sent out for their work in the world twenty-seven soldiers of the Revolution, two attorney-generals, nearly twenty members of Congress, fifteen senators, seventeen governors, thirty-seven judges, a lieutenant-general, two commodores, twelve professors, four signers of the Declaration, seven cabinet officers, a chief justice, and three presidents of the United States."

If I was tempted at first, as I stood before the brick, barn-like building, to exclaim at its ugliness, my frivolous criticism was abashed, as this phantom procession filed through its doorway, for I too, who am not of their blood, claim a share in their greatness, and salute their names with reverent humility.

Laws, Punishments, and Politics

Laws, Punishments, and Politics.

ye Stocks.

IT is a far cry from Patrick Henry, pouring out defiance against the king, while his listeners as one man echoed his final words, "Liberty or death!" back to the night of the arrival of the English ships in Chesapeake Bay, when the box given under the royal seal was opened, and the names of the council who were to govern Virginia were found within. It would have seemed to the group of men standing about the sacred casket on that April night incredible that, within their province of Virginia in the next century, the authority of the king and the power of all England should be openly and successfully set at defiance. Yet so it came to pass, naturally, gradually and inevitably.

The first settlers in Virginia lived in a political condition which may be described as a communism, subject to a despotism. Their goods were held in a common stock, and they drew their rations from "a common kettel," but all the time they felt the strong arm of royal authority stretched across the Atlantic, to rule their affairs without consent of the governed. Both communism and despotism worked badly for the settlers. The first promoted idleness, the second encouraged dissensions, discontent and tale-bearing, each party to a Colonial quarrel being eager to be the first to run home and lay his side of the story before the King. Sir Thomas Dale changed all this communistic living. "When our people were fed out of the common store," writes one of the earliest settlers, "glad was he who could slip from his labor, or slumber over his taske he cared not how; nay, the most honest among them would hardly take so much true paines in a weeke, as now for themselves they will doe in a day, neither cared they for the increase, presuming that howsoever the harvest prospered, the generall store must maintain them, so that wee reaped not so much corne from the labours of thirtie, as now three or foure doe provide for themselves."

Dale allotted to every man three acres of ground, and compelled each to work both for himself and for the public store. His rule was, on the whole, beneficent though arbitrary; but the settlers constantly suffered from the lack of power to make laws, or arrange their simplest affairs without seeking permission from king and council.

Fortunately, after a few years a radical change was wrought; a change whose importance cannot be overestimated. In 1619 Sir George Yeardley came over as Governor of Virginia. He proclaimed that "those cruel laws by which the Ancient Planters had so long been governed" were now done away with, and henceforth they were to be ruled by English law, like all other English subjects. Nor was this all. Shortly after, followed one of those epoch-making declarations which posterity always wonders not to find printed in italics: "That the planters might have a hande in the governing of themselves, yt was grannted that a general assemblie shoulde be helde yearly once, whereat were to be present, the governor and counsell, with two burgesses from each plantation, freely to be elected by the inhabitants thereof, this assemblie to have power to make and ordaine whatsoever lawes and orders should by them be thought good and profitable for their subsistence."

Thus the same year and almost the same month witnessed two events of deep significance to Virginia, the purchase of the first African slaves, and the establishment of the first free Assembly in America. So strangely are the threads of destiny blended! And thus, while the strife between king and people was just beginning to cast its shadow over England, there was quietly inaugurated here at James City a government essentially "of the people, by the people, and for the people."

The measures they adopted at this first free Assembly, the laws they made, the punishments they imposed, are of little importance. The fact of mighty moment is that they met, and though the scope of their power was limited, to be extended two years later, and though they were afterward to struggle on through varying fortunes to the heights of entire freedom, yet this Assembly of 1619 was forever to be memorable as the germ of representative government on this continent.

In the *Quire* of the old brick church, these Burgesses gathered, twenty-two of them, from James City, Charles City, Henrico, Kiccowtan (now Hampton), Martin-Brandon, Smythe's Hundred, Martin's Hundred, Argall's Gift, Lawne's Plantation, Ward's Plantation, and Flowerda Hundred. First, led by Parson Bucke, they asked God's guidance; and on the principle that heaven helps those who help themselves, they then set themselves to the task of framing laws to take the place of the "Iron Code" which Sir Thomas Dale had brought over from the Netherlands, and which strongly suggested the methods of the Inquisition.

Dale's code declared absence from Sunday services a capital offense. One guilty of blasphemy a second time, was sentenced to have a bodkin thrust through his tongue. A Mr. Barnes, of Bermuda Hundred, having uttered a detracting speech against a worthy gentleman in Dale's time, was condemned to have his tongue run through with an awl, to pass through a guard of forty men, and to be butted by every one of them, and at the head of the troop, knocked down, and footed out of the fort. A woman found guilty as a common scold, was sentenced to be ducked three times from a ship in the James River, and one mild statute declared that any person speaking disgraceful words of any person in the colony, should be tied, hand and foot together, upon the ground, every night for the space of one month. It must be said in excuse for the severities of Dale that he had a turbulent mob to discipline. He himself describes them as gathered in riotous or infected places, persons "so profane, or so riotous and treasonable intendments, that in a parcel of three hundred, not many gave testimony beside their name, that they were Christians." Another point to be remembered in defence of this iron soldier, is that all punishments in those days were such as would seem to us cruel and unwarrantable in proportion to the offence. The gallows in London was never idle. Almost every crime was capital. I read in the story of the Virginia adventurers in the Somer Iles of a desperate fellow who, "being to be arraigned for stealing a Turky, rather than he would endure his triall, secretly conveighed himself to sea in a little boat, and never since was heard of." I feel very confident that this poor "Turky"-stealer would never have tempted those stormy waters in a skiff, had he not known full well that a worse fate than drowning awaited him, if he stayed to stand his trial.

The laws introduced by the House of Burgesses were strict enough, and their punishments sufficiently severe. The statutes enacted against "idlenesse" were so salutary that they would soon have exterminated such a social pest as the modern tramp. The law went even further than forbidding idleness, and undertook to discipline those guilty of any neglect of duty. Thomas Garnett, who was accused by his master of wanton and profligate conduct, " and extreame neglect of his busineſſe" was condemned "to stand fower dayes with his eares nayled to the Pillory, and that he, every of those fower days, should be publiquely whipped."

The humiliation of the criminal was the special end and aim of the punishment. Richard Buckland, for writing a slanderous song concerning Ann Smith, was ordered to stand at the church-door during service with a paper round his hat, inscribed "*Inimicus Libellus*," and afterward to ask forgiveness of God, and also in particular of the defamed Ann Smith. Two convicted sinners were

sentenced to stand in church with white sheets round their shoulders and white wands in their hands.

Throughout the century, the statute-books of Virginia and Maryland show a vindictiveness toward criminals which is out of accord with the degree of civilization existing in the colonies. The crime of hog-stealing is visited with special retributions. It is enacted by the Maryland Assembly that any person convicted as a hog-stealer "shall for the first offence stand in the pillory att the Provincial Court four Compleat Hours, & shall have his eares cropt, & pay treble damages; & for the second time, the offender shall be stigmatized in the forehead with the letter H, and pay treble damages; and for the third offence of Hogg stealing, he or they so offending shall be adjudged as fellons. And the Delinquent shall have noe Benefite of Clergy." In another note in the Maryland archives I find: "Putt to the Vote. Whither a Law bee not necessary Prohibiting Negros or any other servants to keepe piggs, hoggs, or any other sort of Swyne uppon any pretence whatsoever."

Hog-stealing seems to have ranked next to murder as an offence, and to have been punished almost as severely—perhaps on Shylock's principle, that they took life who took the means of livelihood;

and the hog in the early days was the chief wealth and maintenance of the settler.

Superstition, as well as cruelty, played its part in the old criminal processes. The blood-ordeal long survived, and the belief was general that a corpse would bleed beneath the murderer's touch. On one occasion, when a serving-woman in Maryland had died under suspicious circumstances, her fellow-servants were summoned one by one to lay hands on the corpse; but as no blood appeared beneath their touch, the jury declared the woman's death to be the act of God.

On the whole, the inhabitants of the Southern Colonies, excepting always the negroes, were singularly free from superstition. The witchcraft delusion, which played such havoc in New England, never obtained a foothold in the Cavalier Colonies. Grace Sherwood was, it is true, accused in Princess Anne County of being a witch, and sentenced to the test of sinking or floating when thrown into the water; but her case stands out quite alone in the annals of Virginia, whereas the same county records show several suits against accusers as defamers of character. Here we find "Jn° Byrd and Anne his wife suing Jn° Pites" in an action of Defamation; their petition sets forth "that the Defend^t had falsely & Scandalously Defamed them, saying they had rid him along the sea-side & home to his own house, by which kind of Discourse they were Reported & rendered as if they were witches, or in league with the Devill, praying 100£ sterl. Damage with cost. The Deft. for answer acknowledgeth that to his thoughts, apprehension or best knowledge they did serve him soe." The jury found for the defendant, but brought no action against the witches who did serve him so.

In lower Norfolk County the defamer did not escape so easily, for " Whereas Ann Godby, the Wife of Tho. Godby hath contrary to an ord^r of ye Court bearing date in May 1655, concerning some slanders & scandalls cast upon women under ye notion of witches, hath contemptuously acted in abusing & Taking ye good name & Credit of nic^o Robinson's wife, terming her a witche, as by severall deposicons appeares. It is therefore ord^d that ye s^d Tho. Goodby shall pay three hundred pounds of Tob^o & Caske fine for her contempt of ye menconed order (being ye first time) & also pay & defray ye cost of sute together wth ye Witnesses' charges at twenty pounds tob^o p day."

Maryland, too, may boast of an unstained record, and of a vigorous warfare against the persecution. An old record tells how John Washington, Esquire, of Westmoreland County, in Virginia, having made complaint against Edward Prescott, merchant,

"Accusin s^d Prescott of ffelony under the Governm^t of this Province (*i. e.* Maryland) Alleaging how that hee, the s^d Prescott, hanged a Witch on his ship as hee was outward bound from England hither the last yeare. Uppon wch complaynt of the s^d Washington, the Govr caused the s^d Edward Prescott to bee arrested." Prescott admitted that one Elizabeth Richardson was hanged on his ship, outward bound from England, but claimed that John Greene, being the master of the vessel, was responsible, and not he. "Whereupon (standing upon his Justificaon) Proclamacaon was made by the Sheriffe in these very words. O yes, &c. Edward Prescott Prisoner at the Bar uppon suspition of ffelony stand uppon his acquittall. If any person can give evidence against him, lett him come in, for the Prisoner otherwise will be acquitt. And noe one appearing, the Prisoner is acquitted by the Board." Yet, though there is not a single conviction of witchcraft to stain the legal records of Maryland, her statute-book in 1639 declared sorcery, blasphemy and idolatry punishable with death; accessories before the fact to be treated as principals. The accusation of blasphemy or idolatry was always a serious one, and the more so on account of its vagueness. Scant proof was required, and the punishment was severe.

A Virginia article of war enacted that swearing

or drunkenness among the soldiery, at the third offense be punished by riding the wooden-horse for an hour, with a musket tied to each foot, and by asking forgiveness at the next meeting for prayer and preaching. This sentence requiring the offender to ask forgiveness is very common in the pages of the statute books as a sequel to the infliction of punishment. Punishment was still disciplinary. Society was a pedagogue and the criminal a naughty school-boy, who must go down on his knees in a proper state of humility before he can be pardoned.

After Bacon's Rebellion, the rebels were sentenced to go through this form of begging forgiveness with a halter round the neck, as a symbol of the right of the Governor to hang them all if he saw fit. One William Potts, being of a haughty spirit, or perhaps possessed of a grim sense of humor, wore round his neck instead of the hempen halter, "a Manchester binding," otherwise a piece of tape. But the jest, if jest it were, was not apparently appreciated by the authorities, for it appears that the Sheriff was straightway deputed to see "that said Potts performe the Law." On the whole, the "said Potts" must have thought himself fortunate, for trifling with magistrates was sternly dealt with in his day, and *answering back* by no means tolerated.

THE COLONIAL CAVALIER.

From the times of Dale onward, a great many statutes were enacted, designed to silence women's tongues. An old Virginia law runs: "Whereas oftentimes many brabling women often slander and scandalize their neighbors, for which their poore husbands are often brought into chargeable and vexatious suits and cast in great damages," it is enacted that all women found guilty of the above offence be sentenced to ducking. The punishment was undoubtedly successful for the time— that is, while the criminal was under water; but it is hard to believe that bad tempers or gossiping habits were permanently cured by the ducking-stool. This curious implement of discipline may still be seen in the old prints. It consists of a chair bound to the end of a long board, which, when released on the land side, plunged the occupant of the chair under water as many times as the magistrate or "her poore husband" required.

Near the court-house, in every town, stood a ducking-stool, a whipping-post, a pillory, and a pair of stocks. In the pillory the criminal stood on a raised platform, with his hands and head thrust through a board on the level with his shoulders, in helpless ignominy. At Queenstown a man found guilty of selling short measure was compelled to stand thus for hours, with the word *cheat* written on his back, while the populace pelted him with stones and eggs. The stocks, while equally ignominious, were somewhat more comfortable, since the malefactor was seated on a bench with his hands and feet pinioned by the jointed planks before him. These were mild forms of punishment. For serious offences, far harsher methods were adopted. Ears were cropped from bleeding heads, hands and feet were cut off, or the offender was sentenced to whipping at the cart's tail, whereupon he was tied to the back of a cart, slowly driven through the town, and thus flogged, as he went, by the common executioner. A not unusual punishment was branding the cheek, forehead, or shoulder with the first letter of the crime committed—as R., for running away; P., for perjury, or S. L., for Seditious Libel. Indeed, the man who escaped with his life from the hands of colonial justice, might count himself fortunate, though he were condemned to go through the remainder of his existence minus a hand, a foot, or an ear; or to have the ignominy of his sentence written on his face for all to read; for sterner punishment than any of these was possible.

Death itself was meted out not infrequently, and the barbarities of drawing and quartering in some instances, fortunately rare, added horror to punishment, and the statistics we find quite calmly set down make the blood run cold.

At a Court held for Goochland County the ninth day of
  October Anno Domi MDCCXXXIII for laying the
  County levey.

Present:

> John ffleming, Daniel Sfoner, Tarlton ffleming,
>   George Payne, William Cabbell, James Skelton,
>   Gent. Justices.

Goochland County..........................Dr. Tobacco.
....

To Thomas Walker & Joseph Dabbs sub-sherifs for a mistake in the levey in 1732.............	10
To Do. for going to Williamsburg for a Comission of Oyer & Terminer to try Champion, Lucy, Valentine, Sampson, Harry & George, Negros 90 miles going at 2lb and 90 miles returning at 2lb p. mile................	360
To Do. for sumoning the Justices and attending the Court for the tryal of the said Negros...	200
To Do. for Executing Champion & Valentine, 250lb each...................................	500
To Do. for providing Tarr, burying the trunk, cutting out the quarters a Pott, Carts & horses carrying and setting up the heads & quarters of the two Negros at the places mentioned by order of Court.....................	2000

And this was in our own country, only a century and a half ago!

A Maryland statute enumerates among capital offences: manslaughter, malicious trespass, forgery, receiving stolen goods, and "stealth of one's self"—which is the unlawful departure of a servant out of service or out of the colony without the consent of his master or mistress—"offender to suffer pains of death by hanging except the offender can read clerk-like, and then he shall lose his hand, and be burned in the hand or forehead with a hot iron, and forfeit his lands at the time of the offense committed." This test of ability to read— "*legit aut non legit?*"—was manifestly a clause inserted to favor the clergy, and so woven into the tissue of mediæval law, that the Reformation had been powerless to unravel it.

It is noticeable that the economical planters wisely preferred those forms of punishment, which cost the State nothing but the services of the constable and the executioner, to the confinement in prison, which involved the support of the criminal at public expense. Prisons, of course, existed almost from the beginning. In the Maryland archives of 1676, I read that "Capt Quigly brought into this house the act for Building the State House and prisson at St Maries, and desires to know what manner of Windowes the house shall have." It is at length decided accordingly by the Assembly "that the windowes are to bee of Wood with substanciall Iron barres and th^t the wood of the frame of the Windowes be layd in Oyle." For the safer guarding of the prisoners, it is also directed that the windows, which were to be only twenty by thirty inches in size, be protected by "Three Iron Barres upright, and two athwart."

The prisons found little occupation as compared with the pillory and the whipping-post. The latter was the common corrector of drunkenness, which was a too frequent offence in those old days in the Cavalier Colonies, when the gentry sipped their madeira over the polished dining-table and the poor man mixed his toddy in his noggin of pewter or wood. All men drank, and most men drank too much. Wines played an important part in the colonial imports. A Virginia statute of 1645 fixed the price of canary and sherry at thirty pounds of tobacco, madeira and "Fyall" at twenty pounds, while aqua-vitæ and brandy ran up to forty. A few years later Master George Fletcher, his heirs and executors, were granted by statute, the sole right to brew in wooden vessels for fourteen years. Maryland laid a tax upon "Rhume, Perrie, Molasses, Sider, Quince Drink or Strong Beer Imported, each 5 lbs tob. per gal."

The State, having made a handsome profit from the selling of all these wines and "hot waters," straightway became very virtuous against the poor wight who took too much. He was sentenced to the joys of the whipping-post, or to be laid in the stocks, or to pay a fine; thus again making liquor pay a revenue to the State. We have an amusing description of what constitutes drunkenness, from a Colonial Dogberry of the seventeenth century, who sapiently observes: "Now, for to know a drunken man the better, the Scripture describes them to stagger and reel to and fro; And so, where the same legs which carry a man into the house can not bring him out again, it is a sufficient sign of drunkenness." The difficulty in convicting these offenders with two pairs of legs, lay in the general sentiment of the community, that after all there was no great harm in taking a little too much of so good a thing as liquor.

The same public sentiment protected duelling, which was under the ban of the statute-books; but these old laws show the futility of attempting to legislate far in advance of public opinion. The law opposed it, but the prevailing sentiment sustained it. The number of duels fought at the South in colonial times has been grossly over-estimated, but they were fought; and the general feeling in regard to the practice was accurately expressed by Oglethorpe of Georgia, that typical Cavalier and true gentleman of the old school, who, when asked if he approved of duelling, made answer, "Of course a man must protect his honor." This curious notion that a man's honor was a vague but very sensitive article, worn about the person, and capable of being injured by any brawler who chanced to jostle against it at an "ordinary," or any vagabond who wished to pick a quarrel with his betters on the road, was a relic of feudal days, when hostile factions met and fought at every corner; and the Colonial Cavalier held to it loyally, never asking himself why or wherefore. This theory, which makes the individual and not the State the avenger of insult and injury, found its logical climax in the methods adopted by Colonel Charles Lynch, a Virginia planter before the Revolution, and the author of a quick and simple form of law called by his name, and very popular still, though, to do him justice, it must be said that his followers have carried his principles further than their author intended. He never took life, but aimed simply to vindicate his own honor and that of his country by inflicting lashes on those who differed with him politically, and thought he did God service when he strung up suspected Tories, and forced them to shout "Liberty forever!"

Thus our study of the lawmaking and lawbreaking records has brought us all the way from that House of Burgesses sitting at James Cittie in 1619—their hearts full of loyalty to his Majesty King James the First, and full of gratitude for the slender liberties he has seen fit to loan rather than grant them—to the brink of the Revolution, to parties of the Crown and of the people, to the hall in the Virginia Capitol where the Assembly is boiling with wrath and defiance against George the Third and his ministers, who have dared to insult the rights and liberties of a free people. It is a mighty transformation to have been brought about in a century and a half. The Southern Colonies did not give up their allegiance without a bitter struggle of reason against sentiment, a struggle which New England never knew; but at length the loyalty which had bowed down to fallen royalty at Breda and yielded Charles II. so early a recognition that he quartered the arms of Virginia with those of England, France, and Scotland, and spoke of it as the Old Dominion—at last, this generous, faithful, confiding loyalty had been outraged past endurance. But still the old traditions lingered. Gen. John Mason says: "So universal was the idea that it was treason and death to speak ill of the king, that I even now remember a scene in the garden at Springfield, when my father's family were spending the day there on a certain Sunday, when I must have been very small. Several of the children having collected in the garden, after hearing in the house among our elders many complaints and distressing forebodings as to this oppressive course towards our country, we were talking the matter over in our own way, and I *cursed* the King, but immediately begged and obtained the promise of the others not to tell on me."

Yet at this moment, when the young rebel was trembling in the garden for the effects of his awful temerity, America was already on the eve of the outbreak which severed her forever from the King and the Kingdom of Great Britain. The allegiance of the loyal colonies could not have fallen so suddenly, but for the long years of sapping and mining which had gone on silently, yet surely, doing their work.

From the time of the thrusting out of Sir John Harvey and his return, backed by the authority of Charles the First, there had been a war waged by proxy between king and people. The governors represented tyranny, and the Assembly opposed each encroachment. Eye to eye they stood, like wrestlers, neither side yielding a point without a struggle, yet both expressing equal loyalty and love for the King, and equal reverence for his authority. Virginia long preserved "an after-dinner allegiance" to the Crown even when she openly defied its policy. Virginians drank his Majesty's health, wiped their lips, and imprecated his Majesty's Navigation Acts. If their political creed bound them to the fiction that the King could do no wrong, they cherished no such delusion concerning his deputies.

When Sir William Berkeley, as despotic at heart as his Stuart master, undertook to play the tyrant in Virginia, the country blazed out into a rebellion, which died only with the death of Nathaniel Bacon, its leader. Bacon was a rebel, but a rebel of the type of Washington and Patrick Henry—one who believed in the motto which Jefferson engraved on his seal, "Rebellion against tyrants is obedience to God." What vigor and eloquence are thrown into his proclamations! They belong to the brightest pages of American literature. Read but the opening of

"NATHANIEL BACON ESQ'R, HIS MANIFESTO CONCERNING THE PRESENT TROUBLES IN VIRGINIA.

"If vertue be a sin, if Piety be giult, all the Principles of morality goodness and Justice be perverted, Wee must confesse That those who are now called Rebells may be in danger of those high imputations, Those loud and severall Bulls would affright Innocents and render the defence of o^r Brethren and the enquiry into o^r sad and heavy oppressions, Treason. But if there bee, as sure there is, a just God to appeal too, if Religion and Justice be a sanctuary here, If to plead ye cause of the oppressed, If sincerely to aime at his Mat^ies Honour and the Publick good without any reservation or by Interest, If to stand in the Gap after soe much blood of o^r dear Brethren bought and sold, If after the losse of a great part of his Maties Colony deserted and dispeopled, freely with o^r lives and estates to indeavor to save the remaynders bee Treason, God Almighty Judge and lett guilty dye. But since wee cannot in o^r hearts find one single spott of Rebellion or Treason or that wee have in any manner aimed at the subverting ye setled Government or attempting of the person of any either magistrate or private man not with standing the severall Reproaches and Threats of some who for sinister ends were disaffected to us and censured o^r ino[cent] and honest designes, and since all people in all places where wee have yet bin can attest o^r civill, quiet, peaseable behaviour farre different from that of Rebellion and tumultuous persons, let Trueth be bold and all the world know the real Foundations of pretended giult."

When this ardent and impetuous nature was vanquished as alone it could be vanquished—by death—Berkeley might, by judicious magnanimity, have healed the wounds of civil war; but, instead, he pursued the conquered rebels with a malignant perseverance, which seemed to grow by what it fed on. "Mr. Drummond," he said ironically to a follower of Bacon brought to him as a prisoner, "you are very welcome! I am more glad to see you than any man in Virginia. You shall be hanged in half an hour."

Twenty-three leaders of this rebellion were thus executed before Berkeley stayed the bloody hand of his vengeance. "The old fool," quoth the King, "hath taken more lives in that naked country, than I for my father's murder!"

Bacon's death remains one of the mysteries of history. Some said he died of miasma in the Virginia swamps; some hinted that his foes poisoned his food, so sudden and mysterious was his ending; and lest Berkeley's revenge should extend to insulting the very corpse of his foe, Bacon's followers buried him with the greatest secrecy, and no man knoweth the resting place of this first colonial champion of popular rights. But the spirit of popular liberty did not die with Bacon, nor vice-royal tyranny with Berkeley. Culpeper, Howard, and a score of others came over from England, one after another, all differing on many points of provincial policy, but united in the determination to fill their own pockets and the royal exchequer by means of colonial revenue. "Lord Colepepper," commented Beverley, "reduced the greatest perquisite of his place to a certainty, which before was only gratuitous; that is, instead of the masters of ships making presents of Liquors or provisions toward the Governor's housekeeping, as they were wont to do, he demanded a certain amount of money, remitting that custom." Such petty exactions as this were a dangerous experiment with a vehement and high-spirited people, who were willing to *give* much, but to *yield* nothing.

The justice and moderation of Spotswood's government held back the tide of popular revolt for some time, and the French and Indian War roused a final flicker of loyalty to the mother-country; but England's success in that struggle cost her the American provinces. When Quebec surrendered to Wolfe's troops, and the French force was withdrawn from Canada, the Comte de Vergennes prophesied the coming revolution against England. "The colonies," said he, "will no longer need her protection. She will call on them to contribute toward supporting the burdens they have helped to bring on her, and they will answer by striking off all dependence."

In 1768 affairs looked stormy in Virginia, and Lord Botetourt was sent over to prophesy smooth things and allay popular irritation, without committing the government by definite promises. The man was well chosen for the task. Junius described him as a cringing, bowing, fawning, sword-bearing courtier. Horace Walpole said his graciousness was enamelled on iron. He came, he saw, he conquered Virginia in a bloodless victory, but Virginia did not stay conquered. When the colonists presented an address which he was pleased to consider insubordinate, Botetourt dissolved the Assembly; but they retired to a private house, elected Peyton Randolph moderator, and prepared and signed a resolution to abstain from all merchandise taxed by Parliament.

The beginning of the end was at hand. The farce of the repeal of the Stamp Act and its reimposition went on. Botetourt went home, and Lord Dunmore, the last of the hated race of governors, came over. His imbecile policy, at once timid and tyrannous, hastened the march of events, but the end was inevitable. "Colonies," said Turgot, "are like fruits, which cling to the tree only till they ripen." So the event proved in America—Virginia and Massachusetts, Maryland and Rhode Island, travelling by different roads, reached the same point of determination at any cost to throw off the yoke of British oppression. Henceforth they were to be no more provincials, but patriots; and Cavalier and Puritan struck hands in the hearty good-will of a common cause.

Sickness and Death

SICKNESS and DEATH.

PIONEER life is all very well when the adventurer is in high health and spirits; but when sickness comes, he must be stout of heart indeed if he does not sigh for the comforts of a civilized home. The poor settlers had a sorry time of it in that first fatal summer on the banks of the James, when they breathed in malaria from the marshes and drank the germs of fever and "fluxes" in the muddy water. "If there were any conscience in men," wrote gallant George Percy, "it would make their hearts bleed to hear the pitiful murmurings and outcries of our sick men, without relief, every day and night for the space of six weeks; some departing out of the world, many times three or four in a night, in the morning their bodies trailed out of their cabins, like dogs, to be buried."

The adventurers profited by the lesson of these troublous times; for as soon as the settlement was fairly re-established under Dale, they set to work upon a hospital. On the river opposite Henrico, they put up "a guest-house for ye sicke people, a high seat and wholesome aire," and christened the place, *Mount Malado*. The chronicles are provokingly silent as to any details of this first American sanitorium. They say nothing of its arrangements, its comforts, or its conveniences. We do not know even the names of those who shared its rude shelter, or of the physicians who treated them. From time to time the mention of some doctor is interwoven with the history of the colonists, but he passes as a pale shadow, with none of the character and substance of the gallant captains, the doughty burgesses, and the tipsy parsons. Doctor Bohun, who is described as "brought up amongst the most learned Surgeons and Physitions in Netherlands," came over and stayed with the settlers for a while, but Lord La Warre carried him off as his medical adviser to the "Western Iles," that his Lordship's gout might be "asswaged by the meanes of fresh dyet, especially Oranges and Limons, an undoubted remedie for that disease"; and a little later the good doctor perished in a sea-fight with Spaniards on the ship *Margaret and John*. Dr. Simons' name is signed to one of the histories, but he too fades away and leaves no trace, and a Dr. Pot has survived only through honorable mention, as "our worthy physition."

Either the country was too healthy, or the inhabitants too poor to encourage immigration among doctors, for they were few and far between, and we find men of other trades acting in the capacity of physician. There was Captain Norton, for instance, "a valiant, industrious gentleman adorned with many good qualities besides Physicke and Chirurgery, which for the publicke good, he freely imparted to all *gratis*, but most bountifully to ye poore."

It was common for barbers to combine the use of the knife with that of the razor, and for the apothecary to prescribe, as well as mix, his own drugs. Colonel Byrd writes that in Fredericksburg, "besides Col. Willis, who is the top man of the place, there are only one merchant, a tailor, a smith, an ordinary-keeper, and a lady who acts both as doctress and coffee-house keeper." A list of prominent citizens in Baltimore in the eighteenth century, includes a barber, two carpenters, a tailor, a parson, and an inn-keeper, but no doctor; unless we reckon as such Dame Hughes and Dame Littig, who are registered as midwives.

The isolation of plantation life made it doubly difficult to depend on doctors, and as a result, each family had its own medicine-chest, and its own recipes and prescriptions handed down from generation to generation, and brought oftentimes from across the sea. Herbs played an important part in the pharmacopœia, both because they were easily obtained, and because tradition endowed them with mysterious virtues. An old medical treatise assures its readers that "Nature has stamped on divers plants legible characters to discover their uses"; that baldness may be cured by hanging-moss, and freckles by spotted plants. Ragwort, and periwinkle, and Solomon's Seal all had their special merits; but sage was prime favorite, and its votary declares it a question how one who grows it in his garden and uses it freely can ever die. Next to ease of preparation, the prime requisite of a medicine was strength. Violent purges and powerful doses of physic or of "The Bark" were always in favor. The simple ailments of childhood were dosed with such abominations as copperas and pewter-filings, and these unhappy infants were fed on beverages of snake-root or soot-tea. One vile compound, common as it was odious, was *snail pottage,* made of garden shell-snails washed in small beer, mixed with earth-worms, and then fried in a concoction of ale, herbs, spices, and drugs.

Yet our ancestors knew how to brew good-tasting things. The letter book of Francis Jerdone, of Yorktown, Virginia, records under date 1746, "A receit how to make Burlington's Universal Balsam.

Balsam Peru	1 oz.
Best Storax	2 oz.
Benjamin, impregnated with sweet Almonds	3 oz.
Alloes Succatrinx	½ oz.
Myrrh Elect	½ oz.
Purest Frankincense	½ oz.
Roots of Angelica	½ oz.
Flowers of St. John Wort	½ oz.

One pint of the best Spirit of Wine.

To be bottled up and Set in the Sun for 20 or 30 days together, to be shaken twice or thrice a day. Take about 30 drops going to bed in Tea made of pennyroyal, Balm or Speer mint."

This prescription has the great defect of being too good, and might have a tendency to tempt the young to acquire the disease in order to be treated to the remedy. *Angelic Snuff* was another agreeable medicament, warranted to cure all head troubles and help the palsy, megrims, deafness, apoplexy, and gout. What a pity that only the name of this cure remains to our generation, whose megrims alone would empty so many boxes of the invaluable snuff!

The early settlers could, if they would, have learned some useful lessons in the treatment of disease from the Indians, who at least understood making the skin share the work of the stomach. A primitive, but very effective, way of treating fevers and similar ailments among the natives was by the sweating-oven. The Indian patient would creep into these mounds, under which a fire had been lighted, while the medicine-man poured on water from above, creating a mighty steam, in which the patient would continue till even Indian fortitude could hold out no longer, when he would crawl out, and, rushing down to the nearest stream, plunge headlong into its cold waters. All this process was, of course, performed amid incantations as mysterious to the whites as the phraseology of a modern physician to a savage.

This treatment was more in harmony with modern ideas than the methods which prevailed among the English. When the two Spotswood boys were sent across the sea to Eton, to school, they spent their vacations with their aunt, Mrs. Campbell, who writes to their landlady at the end of their stay: "I am very Sorry, Madam, to send them back with such bad coughs, though I have nursed Jack who was so bad that we were obliged to Bleed him, and physick him, that he is much better. I can't judge how they got them (the coughs). My son came home with one, and has never been out of the house but once since, and these children have always laid warm, and lived constantly in the house." These poor little victims of the coddling system would probably have recovered rapidly in the steam-bath of their native

Virginia and the fresh air of her pine forests, but instead, they are sent back from one hothouse to another. "I beg," adds their affectionate, but misguided aunt, "that they may be kept in a very warm room, and take the drops I send every night, and the pectoral drink several times a day, and that they eat no meat or drink anything but warm barley water and lemon juice, and, if Aleck increases, to get Blooded." It is a great relief, and something of a surprise, to learn that Aleck and his brother John lived to come back to America and figure in the Revolution. Perhaps their recollections of the dosing and "blooding" they received in their youth threw additional energy into their opposition to the oppression of England.

Cupping, leeching, and all sorts of blood-letting were the chief dependence in olden times in all cases of fever. The free use of water, now so universal, would then have been thought fatal. The poor patient dreaded the doctor more than the disease, and often with reason. Anæsthetics, that best gift of science to a suffering world, were unknown, and surgery was vivisection with the victim looking on, conscious and quivering.

The doctor in the Cavalier Colonies was regarded with almost as much suspicion as the parson—as a cormorant, ready and anxious to prey on the community, and to be held in check by all the severities of the law. Virginia in 1657 passed statutes regulating surgeons' fees. In 1680 physicians were compelled to declare under oath the value of their drugs, and the court allowed them fifty per cent advance on the cost. If any physician was found guilty of neglecting a patient, he was liable to fine and punishment.

In the eighteenth century, still stricter laws were framed, "because of surgeons, apothecaries and unskillful apprentices who exacted unreasonable fees, and loading their patients with medicine." The fees fixed by this statute are "one shilling per mile and all medicines to be set forth in the bill." The price for attending a common fracture is set down at two pounds, and double the sum for attending a compound fracture. A university degree entitled the practitioner to higher charges, but its posssesion was rare. Most doctors were trained up in the offices of older men as apprentices, pounders of drugs, and cleaners of instruments, as the old painters began by preparing paints and brushes for the master.

A modern man of science would smile at the titles of the old medical works solemnly consulted by our forbears. "A Chirurgicall Booke" sounds interesting, and "The Universall Body of Physick"; but they are not so alluring as "The Way to Health, long life and Happiness," nor so attractive to the ignorant as "The Unlearned Keymiss." Perhaps the struggling physicians and chirurgians who doctored by these old books and their common-sense, helped as many and harmed no more than the chemist of to-day, with his endless pharmacopœia of coal-tar products, tonics, and stimulants; or the specialist who, instead of "the Whole Body of Physick," devotes himself wholly to a single muscle, or nerve-ganglion.

In spite of the chill of popular disfavor and of the difficulties of professional training, good and noble men worked on faithfully at the business of helping the sick and suffering in the colonies. The Maryland annals tell of a Dr. Henry Stevenson, who built him a house near the York road so elegant, that the neighbors called it "Stevenson's Folly." If there was any envy in their hearts, however, it changed to gratitude and admiration when the small-pox appeared in their midst, and the large-hearted doctor turned his mansion into a hospital. It is hard for us who live after the days of Jenner, to appreciate the terror of the word *small-pox*. In the eighteenth century pitted faces were the rule. Fathers feared to send their sons to England, so prevalent was the disease there. An old journal advertises: "Wanted, a man between twenty and thirty years of age, to be a footman and under-butler in a great family; he must be of the Church of England, and have had the small-pox in the natural way."

This enlightened Dr. Stevenson, of Stevenson's Folly, made Maryland familiar with the process of inoculation, which antedated vaccination. He advertises in *The Maryland Gazette* of 1765 that he is ready to inoculate "any gentlemen that are pleased to favor him in that way," and that his fees are two pistoles for inoculating, and twenty shillings per week board, the average cost to each patient being £5 14s.

Ryland Randolph writes to his brother at a time when inoculation is still a new thing: "I wrote to my Mother for her consent to be inoculated for the small-pox, but since see that she thinks it a piece of presumption. When you favor me with a line, pray let me have your opinion of it!"

In 1768, we find the authorities at *William and Mary* resolving "that an ad. be inserted in the Gazette to inform the Publick that the College is now clear of small-pox," and a few days later they frame another resolution that "fifty pounds be allowed to Dr. Carter for his care and attendance on those afflicted with said disorder at the College."

Meanwhile the colonists had not followed up their good beginning at Mount Malado. Hospitals had not grown with the growth of the community. Doctors had none of the advantages of the study of surgery and medicine which are given by the hospital system, but the sick were tenderly cared for, nevertheless. In Jefferson's notes on the advantages enjoyed by the Virginians, he speaks of: "their condition too when sick, in the family of a good farmer where every member is emulous to do them kind offices, where they are visited by all the neighbors, who bring them the little rarities which their sickly appetites may crave, and who take by rotation the nightly watch over them, without comparison better than in a general hospital where the sick, the dying and the dead are crammed together in the same room, and often in the same bed." When we read the accounts of hospitals in the eighteenth century, antiseptics unknown, and even ordinary cleanliness uncommon, we can readily agree with the conclusion that "Nature and kind nursing save a much greater proportion in our plain way, at a smaller expense, and with less abuse."

Every wind that swept the sick-room in those colonial farm houses, brought balm from the pines, or vigor from the sea. Three thousand miles of uncontaminated air stretched behind them and before. This pure, balmy, bracing air cured the sick, and kept the well in health, in spite of general disregard of hygiene, which prevailed almost universally, especially in all matters of diet. "We may venture to affirm," exclaims a horrified Frenchman, fresh from the land of scientific cookery, "that if a premium were offered for a regimen most destructive to the teeth, the stomach and the health in general, none could be desired more efficacious for these ends than that in use among this people. At breakfast they deluge the stomach with a pint of hot water slightly impregnated with tea, or slightly tinctured, or rather coloured with coffee; and they swallow, without mastication, hot bread half-baked, soaked in melted butter, with the grossest cheese and salt or hung beef, pickled pork, or fish, all which can with difficulty be dissolved. At dinner, they devour boiled pastes, called absurdly puddings, garnished with the most luscious sauces. Their turnips and other vegetables are floated in lard or butter. Their pastry is nothing but a greasy paste imperfectly baked."

The entire day, according to this cheerful observer, is passed in heaping one indigestible mass on another, and spurring the exhausted stomach to meet the strain, by wines and liquors of all sorts. The population who lived on such a diet, ought to have died young, to point the moral of the hygienist; but Nature pardons much to those who live in the open air. If digestions were taxed, nerves remained unstrained. Even in our age of hurry and bustle, anything like nervous prostration is rare, south of Mason and Dixon's line. The soft air and the easy life soothe the susceptibilities, and oil the wheels of existence. It is for these reasons, perchance, that the records of the burying-grounds in the Southern colonies show such a proportion of names of octogenarians who had survived to a ripe old age, in spite of hot breads washed down with hotter liquors.

These burying-grounds of the old South are robbed of much of the dreariness of their kind by being generally laid out in close proximity to the living world, as if the chill of the tomb were beaten back by the fire-light falling on it from the familiar hearth-stone close at hand. It is a comfort to think of genial Colonel Byrd, who loved so well the good things of this world, resting under a monument which duly sets forth his virtues, on the edge of the garden at Westover, beneath an arbor screened only by vines from the door where he passed in and out for so many years.

Hugh Jones, that conservative son of the church, lamented that the Virginians did not prefer to lie in the church-yard for their last long sleep. "It is customary," he says regretfully, "to bury in garden, or orchards, where whole families lye interred together, in a spot, generally handsomely enclosed, planted with evergreens, and the graves kept decently. Hence, likewise, arises the occasion of preaching funeral sermons in houses where, at funerals, are assembled a great congregation of neighbors and friends; and if you insist on having the service and ceremony at church, they'll say they will be without it, unless performed after their own manner."

Here we have a flash of the spirit of resistance to undue encroachments from church or state, which flamed up half a century later into open revolt. There is something touching in this clinging to the home round which so many memories cluster, in this desire to lay the dead there close to all they had loved, and when their own time came, to lie down beside them under the shadow of the old walls which had sheltered their infancy, and youth, and age.

If the burying-grounds were cheerful, still more so were the funerals. They partook, in fact, of the nature of an Irish wake. Wine was freely drunk, and funeral baked meats demolished, while the firing of guns was so common that many asked by will that it be omitted, as friends to-day are "kindly requested to omit flowers."

The funeral expenses of a gentleman of Baltimore town in the eighteenth century were somewhat heavy, as any one may judge from an itemized account preserved to us, which includes: "Coffin

£6 16s, 41 yds. crape, 32 yds. black Tiffany, 11 yds. black crape, 5½ broadcloth, 7½ yards of black Shaloon, 16½ yds. linen, 3 yds. sheeting, 3 doz. pairs men's black silk gloves, 2 doz. pairs women's do., 6 pairs men's blk. gloves (cheaper), 1 pr. women's do., black silk handkerchiefs, 8½ yards calamanco, mohair and buckram, 13½ yds. ribbon, 47½ lbs. loaf sugar, 14 doz. eggs, 10 oz. nutmegs, 1½ pounds alspice, 20⅝ gallons white wine, 12 bottles red wine, 10⅜ gallons rum." The total cost of these preparations amounts to upward of fifty pounds sterling, besides the two pounds to be paid to Dame Hannah Gash and Mr. Ireland for attendance, while ten shillings additional were allowed for "coffin furniture."

When a Thomas Jefferson, ancestor of *the* Thomas Jefferson, died in Virginia in 1698, his funeral expenses included the items:

To Benj. Branch for a Mutton for the funerall	60lbs. tobacco.
To Ann Carraway and Mary Harris for mourning Rings..........................	£1
To Sam'll Branch for makeing ye coffin....	10^s
For plank for ye coffin.......................	2^s 6^d

The list of expenses closes with unconscious satire, thus: "Previous item—to Dr. Bowman for Phisick, 60 lbs. tobacco," showing that every arrangement for the taking under was complete.

THE COLONIAL CAVALIER.

These inventories and wills cast wonderful sidelights on the manners and customs of "ye olden tyme." To our age, accustomed to endless post-mortem litigation, there is a refreshing simplicity in these old documents, which seem to take for granted that it is only necessary to state the wishes of the testator. Richard Lightfoote, ancestor of the Virginia Lightfoots, who made his will in 1625, "in the first yeare of the raigne of our Soveraigne Lord King Charles," feeling perhaps a little fearful of disputes among his heirs, appoints Thomas Jones "to bee overseer herof, to see the same formed in all things accordinge to my true meaninge; hereby requestinge all the parties legatees aforenamed to make him judge and decider of all controversies which shall arise between them or anie of them." But there is no record that the services of Thomas Jones were needed as mediator, and when Jane Lightfoote, his wife, makes her will, she goes about it in a still more childlike and trustful fashion.

She leaves her "little cottage pott" to one, and her "little brasse pan" to another. No object is too trifling to be disposed of individually. The inventory of Colonel Ludlow, who departed this life in 1660, is a curious jumble of things small and large. Here we have "one rapier, one hanger, and black belt, three p'r of new gloves and one p'r of horn buckskin gloves, one small silver Tankard, one new silver hat-band, two pair of silver breeches buttons, one wedding Ring, one sealed Ring, a pcell of sweet powder and 2 p'r of band strings," besides which is specially mentioned: "Judge Richardson to ye Wast in a picture," valued at fifty pounds of tobacco. In addition to these, Colonel Ludlow died possessed of "12 white servants and ten negroes, 43 cattle, 54 sheep and 4 horses."

The favorite testimonial of affection to survivors was the mourning ring or seal. These gifts figure in almost every will we examine, one mentioning a bequest of money for the purchase of "thirty rings for relatives." The keepsakes were carefully cherished, and the survivors in turn set up the memorial tablet, or carved the tombstone, or presented some piece of plate to the parish church, to keep fresh the name and memory of the deceased. In Christ Church, at Norfolk, is an old Alms Bason marked with a Lion Passant and a Leopard's Head crowned, in the centre a coat of arms, three Griffins' heads erased, and the inscription:

> "The gift of Capt. Whitwell in
> memory of Mrs. Whitwell who was
> intered in the church at Norfolk,
> ye 8th of March, 1749."

The same church owns a flagon with a crest, "a demi-man ppr-crowned in dexter three ostrich feathers," given by Charles Perkins as a memorial to his wife, Elizabeth, who died in 1762.

It was a pleasant thought thus to renew the memory of departed friends by flagon, and plate, and alms-basin—a wiser way, one feels, than the carving of long epitaphs on gloomy stones surmounted by skull and cross-bones. How often, as we read these dreary tributes, we long for some shock of truth to nature, among all this decorous conventionalism! What tales these old colonial graveyards might have told us if they would! Here lie men who, perchance, supped with Shakespeare, or jested with Jonson and Marlow at *The Mermaid*.

Here rest gallants who closed round the royal standard on the fatal field of Marston Moor, or danced at Buckingham Palace with the free and fair dames of the merry court of Charles Second after the Restoration; but not a word of all this appears on the stones that represent them. Their epitaphs plaster them over with all the Christian virtues, and obscure their individuality as completely as the whitewash brushes of Cromwell's soldiers obliterated the dark, quaintly carved oak of the cathedrals. *De mortuis nil nisi bonum* makes churchyard literature very dull reading, when it should be the most interesting and instructive in the world. Had the stones set forth the lives of those who rest beneath, we might learn much of such a man as Sir George Somers, whose strange experiences on the *Sea-Venture* and his adventures on the Bermudas make me want to know more of him. I want to know what caused the trouble between him and Gates; how he built his cedar ships; how he looked, and walked, and talked; and what manner of man he was, all in all. Instead of gratifying my innocent curiosity, his tombstone in Whitchurch, where he is buried, puts me off with a florid verse of poor poetry, and I am little better helped when I turn to the records of the island where he died. Here Capt. Nathaniel Butler, "finding accidentally" (so runs the old chronicle) "a little crosse erected in a by-place amongst a great many of bushes, understanding there was buried the heart and intrailes of Sir George Somers, hee resolved to have a better memory of so worthy a Souldier than that. So, finding also a great Marble Stone brought out of England, hee caused it to bee wrought handsomely, and laid over the place, which he invironed with a square wall of hewen stone, tombe-like, wherein hee caused to be graven this epitaph he had composed, and fixed it on the Marble Stone and thus it was:

THE COLONIAL CAVALIER.

"In the year 1 6 1 1
Noble Sir George Summers went hence to Heaven
Whose noble, well-tried worth that held him still imploid
Gave him the knowledge of the world so wide.
Hence 't was by heavens decree that to this place
He brought new guests and name to mutual grace.
At last his soule and body being to part,
He here bequeathed his entrailes and his heart."

Even this gives us more information about the dead than most of the epitaphs. They are composed, as a rule, with Jonsonian elaborateness, and might as well be set up over Rasselas, as over those they commemorate.

On the tomb of President Nelson of his Majesty's Council, in the old York churchyard, a pompous inscription announces: "Reader, if you feel the spirit of that exalted ardor which aspires to the felicity of conscious virtue, animated by those consolations and divine admonitions, perform the task and expect the distinction of the righteous man!" The "*distinction of the righteous*" is a delightful phrase, and sets forth the instinctive belief of the Cavalier in aristocracy in heaven.

A Latin inscription was regarded as an appropriate tribute to the learning of the deceased, who, had his ghost walked o' nights, might have needed to brush up his classics to make quite sure of what his survivors were saying about him.

In happy contrast to the frigidity of these epitaphs wherein the dead languages bury their dead, is the verse written by his son over the "Honble Coll. Digges," who died in 1744:

> "Diggs, ever to extremes untaught to bend
> Enjoying life, yet mindful of its end
> In thee the world an happy mingling saw
> Of sprightly humor and religious awe."

How it warms our hearts to find the word *humor* on a gravestone! It takes the chill out of death itself, and inspires us with the hope that this most lovable of traits may stand as good a chance of immortality as Faith, Hope, or Charity.

A brief and business-like epitaph written over Mistress Lucy Berkeley, declares that "She left behind her 5 children viz. 2 Boys and 3 Girls. I shall not pretend to give her full character; it would take too much room for a Grave-stone. Shall only say she never neglected her duty to her Creator in publick or private. She was charitable to the poor, a kind Mistress, Indulgent Mother, and Obedient Wife."

For a parallel to this matron who neglected no duty, "publick or private," we must seek the tomb of a maiden. On the crumbling stone the tribute still survives, and tells that

> "In a Well grounded Certainty of an
> Immortal Resurrection
> Here lyes the Remains of Elizabeth
> the Daughter of
> John and Catharine Washington
> She was a Maiden
> Virtuous without Reservedness
> Wise without Affectation
> Beautiful without Knowing it
> She left this life on the Fifth day of
> Feb^r in the Year MDCCXXXVI in the
> Twentieth Year of her age."

One more epitaph of the Colonial Cavaliers I must quote in full, because it alone, of all I have studied, does give a picture of the man who lies under it. If it praises him too much, it is to be set down to his credit that one who knew him well believed it all; and I for one wish peace to the dust of this gallant old mariner who sailed the seas in colonial days. Here he lies, sunk at his moorings, "one who never struck his flag while he had a shot in the locker; who carried sail in chace till all was blue; in peace whose greatest glory was a staggering topsail breeze; in war to bring his broadside to bear upon the enemy, and who, when signals of distress hove out, never stood his course, but hauled or tacked or wore to give relief, though to a foe; who steered his little bark full fifty annual cruises over life's tempestuous ocean and moored her safe in port at last; where her timbers being crazy, and having sprung a leak in the gale, she went down with a clear hawse. If these traits excite in the breast of humanity that common tribute to the memory of the departed—a sigh—then traveller as thou passest this wreck, let thine be borne upon the breeze which bends the grassy covering of the grave of *Old Job Pray.*"

This stone, like many another we find in these old brick-walled Southern burying-grounds, brings a smile which borders close upon a tear. The very spelling and lettering in these primitive inscriptions seem moss-grown with age, and tell of generations passed away, bearing their manners and customs before them, as Mary Stuart bears her head on the charger in the Abbotsford picture. Here on one crumbling stone we read of a matron who hated strife with a capital "S" and loved peace with a little "p." Here we read the touching little life-history of the young wife of John Page, who "blest her said Husband with a sonn and a Daughter and departed this life, the twelfth day of November, Anno Dom 1702, and in the 20th yeare of her age."

The inscriptions on the oldest tombstones are

undecipherable. The bluestone slab under the ruined arch at Jamestown clasped by the roots of the sycamore was so broken and defaced even when Lossing visited it that nothing remained but the shadowy date, 1608. But in the earliest inscriptions that survive, we are struck by the virile and nervous English. It smacks of "great Eliza's golden day." A fragment of one runs:

> "O Death! all-eloquent, you only prove
> What dust we dote on when 't is man we love."

But finest of all is the noble dirge, sung over Bacon's lifeless body by some one whose name will never now be surely known, since he disguised his identity, prompted by a wise dread of Berkeley's malignant revenge, and states that after Bacon's death "he was bemoaned in these following lines, drawn by the man that waited upon his person as it is said, and who attended his corpse to their burial place." Whoever the writer was, and a high authority designates him as a man named Cotton, dweller at Acquia Creek, it is very sure that no serving-man composed these lines, which are like an echo of the age that gave us Lycidas:

> "Who is't must plead our cause? Nor trump nor drum
> Nor deputations; these, alas! are dumb;
> And can not speak. Our arms, though ne'er so strong,
> Will want the aid of his commanding tongue.

THE COLONIAL CAVALIER.

> "Here let him rest; while we this truth report
> He's gone from hence unto a higher court
> To plead his cause, where he by this doth know,
> Whether to Cæsar he was friend or foe."

These closing words may well form the epitaph written over the Colonial Cavalier. He is gone from hence unto a higher court—gone from this world forever. His open-handed hospitality, his reckless profusion, his chivalry to women, his quick-tempered, sword-thrusting honor, are as obsolete as his lace ruffles, his doublet and jerkin, his buckles and jewels and feathers. We are fallen on a prosaic age, and it is only in our dreams of the past that we conjure up, like a gay decoration against the neutral background of modern life, the figure of "The Colonial Cavalier."

Appendix

List of Authorities

Alden's Collection of American Epitaphs and Inscriptions
Alsop's Character of the Province of Maryland
Anburey's Travels through the Interior Parts of America
Bancroft's History of the United States
Beverley's History and Present State of Virginia
Bozman's History of Maryland
Browne's Maryland
Buck's Old Plate
Burwell Papers, The
Byrd's Westover Manuscripts
Campbell's History of the Colony and Ancient Dominion of Virginia
Chastellux's Travels in North America
Cooke's Virginia
Doyle's English Colonies in America
Fisher's The Colonial Era
Hammond's Leah and Rachel; or, The Two Fruitful Sisters, Virginia and Maryland
Hamor's True Discourse of the Present Estate of Virginia
Hening's Virginia Statutes at Large
Hildreth's History of the United States
Howe's Historical Collections of Virginia
Howell's State Trials
Irving's Life of Washington
Jefferson's Notes on the State of Virginia
Jefferson, Thomas, Life and Letters of
Jones' True Relation of the Present State of Virginia
Lee, Richard Henry, Life and Letters of

APPENDIX.

Lossing's Pictorial Field-Book of the Revolution
McMaster's History of the People of the United States
Madison, Mrs. Dolly, Life and Letters of
Maryland Archives
Magazine of American History
Meade's Old Churches, Ministers, and Families of Virginia
Moore's History of North Carolina
Purchas: His Pilgrimes
Ramsay's History of South Carolina
Ridgely's Annals of Annapolis
Robin, Abbé, New Travels through North America
Rowland's Life of George Mason
Scharf's Chronicles of Baltimore
Smith's General History of Virginia
Smith's True Relation of Virginia
Tyler's Life of Patrick Henry
Tyler's History of American Literature
Virginia Historical Register, Ed. by W. Maxwell
Virginia Magazine of History and Biography
Whitaker's Good Newes from Virginia
William and Mary College Quarterly
Wirt's Life of Patrick Henry

---- Belinda, 67 Boodle, 143
Brooke, 143 Darius, 226
Eddis, 153 Elizabeth, 76
James, 75 Job, 48 Lee, 219
Madison, 219 Mary, 88 Patrick,
217 Robin, 69 Thomson, 88
William, 223
ANBURY, 182 183
ANNE QUEEN OF ENGLAND,
177
ARCHER, 129
ATKINSON Richard, 173
BACON, 52 225 Gen, 53
Madam, 53 Parson, 161
BALLARD Madam, 53
BALTIMORE Lord, 50 100 104
105
BERKELEY, 34 118 225
Edmund, 226 Gov, 79 223
Lady, 52 83 William, 51 53
80
BEVERLY, 26 37
BLACK WILLIAM, 159
BLACKBEARD, 103
BLAIR COMMISSARY, 51 117
BLAND Anna, 88 Col, 215
Sarah, 29 Theodorick, 88
BLEWER Thomas, 205
BOTETOURNT Gov, 157 Lord,
158
BOTETOURT Lord, 157
BOUCHER Jonathan, 161
BRADDOCK, 83 136 Gen, 144
BRANDON, 34
BRAY Madam, 53
BRENT Margaret, 49 Mrs, 49
BROWN, 94
BUCKE MR, 197
BUCKINGHAM, 79
BUCKNER JOHN, 181
BURAS ANNE, 48
BURWELL Becca, 64 66 156
Lewis, 50

BYRD Col, 30 31 45 57 60 63
Evelyn, 60 63
CALVERT Gov, 49 80
CAMM John, 215 218 219 Mr,
215
CAMPBELL Mrs, 87
CARLETON Dudley, 77
CARROLL Charles, 93
CARTER Col, 215 King, 15
CASTLEMAINE Lady, 144
CHARLES I KING OF ?, 79 210
CHARLES II KING OF ?, 78
143
CHARLES KING OF ?, 79
CHARLTON Henry, 194
CHASTELLUX, 33 160
CHEESMAN Edmund, 52
COLEMAN Henry, 194
CORBIN Alice, 65
CORNWALEYS Thomas, 131
COTTON Mr, 194 Rev Mr, 194
CROYDON, 77
CULPEPER LORD, 52
CUSTIS, 69 Master, 93 Parke, 60
Patsy, 162
DALE Lady, 134 Of The
Netherlands, 193 Thomas,
134 197
DANDRIDGE Martha, 60
DARTMOUTH Earl Of, 177
DECHASTELLUX MARQUIS,
70
DEFOE Daniel, 48
DELAMAER Lord, 226
DELAWARRE Lord, 21 196 202
DEREIDEFEL Madame, 106
DERRICOAT William, 119
DOUGHOREGAN, 34
DURAND John, 92
DYER Sarah, 225
EDWARDS Jonathan, 179
FAIRFAX Lord, 37 63 149

FITZHUGH Col, 80 181
  William, 29 115
FORBES Rev Mr, 197
FOREST Mistress, 48
FOSTER MRS, 87
FOX, 217
FRANKLIN, 116 119 Benjamin, 109 Dr, 109
FRIZELL Susan, 170 171
FULLER Thomas, 198
GARZIA Parson, 212
GATES, 100 Thomas, 21
GAY, 206
GEORGE III KING OF ?, 148
GIFFORD Ursula, 49
GLASSCOCKE Robert, 214
GLOUCESTER DUKE OF, 16
GODDARD Mary, 123
GOLIATH, 146
GOOCH Gov, 159
GOODBY Anna, 225 226
GOUCH Gov, 186
GRANDISON Charles, 57
GREENE Gen, 154 Gov, 49
  Katherin, 225 Wm, 225
GWYNNS Nell, 159
HALLAM, 158 159
HAMOR, 22 133 134 Ralph, 21
HANDSLEY Elizabeth, 173
HARRISON Ben, 156 Mr, 213
  Thomas, 213
HEMANS, 50
HENRY, 217 Patrick, 85 154 178 216
HIGGS Lisa, 13
HILL William, 173
HOWELLS, 172
HUNT Master, 192 207
INDIAN Bright-Stream-Between-Two-Hills, 46 King Pamaunche, 128 King Powhatan, 133
  Ottamatomakkin, 47
  Pocahontas, 46 134
  Powhatan, 47 129 134
JAMES I KING OF ENGLAND, 172 173
JAMES KING, 138
JAMES KING OF ENGLAND, 172
JARRATT Devereux, 174
JEFFERSON, 51 64 67 68 96 111 130 154 156 177 184 187
  Tom, 66 155
JOHNSON Sheriff, 173
JONES Hugh, 30 34 156 180
JONSON, 155
JULIUS CAESAR, 226
KEMP Matthew, 202
KNELLER Godfrey, 63
LAWRENCE Richard, 226
LAYDON John, 47
LEE Charles, 150 Col, 219 Rich'd Henry, 219
LEMAYEUR Dr, 91
LEWIS Mr, 215 William, 49
LILIE, 94
LUDWELL Mr, 52 Philip, 52
LYONS, 216 225 Mr, 215
MACDONALD Flora, 58 59
MADEIRA, 161
MADISON, 51 219 Dolly, 88 Mrs, 32
MARSHALL Chief-Justice, 55
MARY OF SCOTLAND, 76
MARY QUEEN OF ?, 16
MASON Col, 162 George, 89 John, 33 Madam, 87 Mrs, 34
MATHER Cotton, 211
MAURY James, 215
MAYNARD Lt, 103
MCCLURG Mrs, 218
MCKEOGN John, 123
MEADE Bishop, 179 201
MERCER Col, 219 James, 219

MINOR Garrett, 203
MODISH Betty, 57
MONTAGUE William, 203
MONTCLARE, 34
MOORE Betsy, 156 Tom, 59
MORRIS Capt, 69 Edward, 121
NEALE Thomas, 115
NEGRO Billy, 176
NELSON Mary, 123
NEWTON Amy, 92
NICHOLAS Betsey, 120
NICHOLSON Capt, 117 Gov, 50 Lady, 51
PACKER Thomas, 76
PAGE Jack, 156 John, 65 Madam, 53 Nancy, 156 Daniel, 117
PAYNE Dolly, 88 Mary, 173
PEPYS Madam, 83 Samuel, 80
PETERBOROUGH Earl Of, 60
PHILLIPSE Mary, 69 84
PHYALL, 161
PITT MR, 218
PORTER John, 225 John Jr, 225
PORY John, 77
POSEY Milly, 162
POTTER Sukey, 156
POWELL Mary, 194
R Belinda, 66
RANDOLPH Betsey, 120 Edmund, 120 John, 178
RATHEL Catherine, 93
REBECCA Lady, 46
RITCHIE Archy, 219
RIVINGTON, 94
ROBIN Abbe, 54
ROBINSON Beverly, 69
ROGERS Stephen, 172
ROLFE, 47 John, 46 169
ROOKES Ralph, 173
ROSE Robert, 208
RUSSELL Richard, 225
SCHARF, 91

SENIS James, 203
SEWELL Mr, 213 214
SHAKESPEARE, 155
SHEPHERD Thomas, 199
SHIRLEY Maj-Gen, 110
SIMMS Thomas, 203
SIR WALTER, 155
SKELTON Martha, 67 Mrs, 68
SMITH, 19 46 47 134 Capt, 128 John, 76 129 Thomas, 115 145 173
SMYTH, 40
SOMER, 100
SPELMAN, 129 130 131
SPOTSWOOD, 41 Gov, 30 57 83 103 148 157 202 210 Lady, 210 Mrs, 30
SPRINGER Col, 200
STEELE, 94
STERNE, 206
STEVENS Frances, 52
STONE Virlinda, 50
SWEENY Charles, 202
SWIFT Dr, 206
SYMPSON Paul, 27
TANNER Danyell, 213 214
TARLETON, 16
TAYLOR Jeremy, 198 John, 203
THEACH John, 103
THOMAS Mr, 57
TILLIT John, 176
TOMKIES Suckie, 119
TRYON Gov, 58 Lady, 58
WAKE Esther, 58
WALTON Mr, 181
WASHINGTON, 37 51 63 69 83 84 89 90 92 93 95 110 136 148 149 154 186 203 George, 156 178 187 Lady, 60
WATKINS George, 172
WESLEY, 217
WESTOVER, 34

WHITAKER, 198 207
    Alexander, 197
WHITE, 143
WHITEFIELD, 178 217
WILFORD T, 27
WILKINS Miss, 55
WILLIAM KING OF ?, 16 Sir,
    223

WINGFIELD, 19 193 Edward
    Maria, 192
WIRT, 217 Mr, 85
WITHERS John, 181
WORMELEY Ralph, 227
WREN Christopher, 30
WYTHE George, 33
YATES Richard, 225
YEARDLEY Gov, 77

www.ingramcontent.com/pod-product-compliance
Lightning Source LLC
Chambersburg PA
CBHW071958220426
43662CB00009B/1184